A Complete Beginner's Guide
Options Relaxing Trading

DAVID CARLI

Option trading involves substantial risk and is not suitable for all investors. Trading options is difficult and requires extensive study. I cannot and will not guarantee that you will not lose money or that you will make money from the information found on this book. Past results do not guarantee future results. You can lose money trading options and the loss can be substantial including more than you invest. Losing trades can occur and will occur in the future. Don't trade with money you can't afford to lose. Only risk capital should be invested since it is possible to lose all of your principal.

Copyright © First edition in May 2024 by David Carli.

All rights reserved. This book or any portion thereof may not be reproduced or used in any manner whatsoever without the express written permission of the publisher except for the use of brief quotations in a book review.

First Printing: 2024

ISBN: 9798332800979

Website: www.tradingwithdavid.com
E-mail: info@tradingwithdavid.com

EDITED

Hannah Hermes
hannahhermes@gmail.com

Contents

Introduction – About the Author 1
Introduction – Preface 2

PART ONE: FEATURES OF OPTIONS

Chapter 1 – The History of Options 5
Chapter 2 – Introduction to Options 9
Chapter 3 – Selling Options 20
Chapter 4 – Options vs. Stocks 24
Chapter 5 – Coverage or Speculation 27

PART TWO: VERTICAL SPREAD

Chapter 6 – Hedging Against the Risk 35
Chapter 7 – Vertical Spread 37
Chapter 8 – Buying a Vertical Spread 45
Chapter 9 – Choose the Right Options 54
Chapter 10 – Stop-Loss Strategies 60
Chapter 11 – Manage a Credit Spread 65

PART THREE: OTHER STRATEGIES

Chapter 12 – Short Iron Condor 71
Chapter 13 – Manage a Short Iron Condor 83

Chapter 14 – Covered Call 90
Chapter 15 – Some Comments 104

PART FOUR: MANAGEMENT

Chapter 16 – Money Management 109
Chapter 17 – Volatility and VIX Index 113
Chapter 18 – Option Assignment 118
Chapter 19 – Open Interest 122
Chapter 20 – Exploit the Acceleration 133
Chapter 21 – Backtesting and Simulation 139
Chapter 22 – Final Conclusions 147

PART FIVEE: APPENDIX

Appendix A – Greeks 153
Appendix B – Web Resources 162
Appendix C – Options Glossary 164

About the Author
Introduction

My journey in the investment and trading world started shortly after I graduated from the University of Pisa, Italy. I then travelled to New York city, USA., where I attended exclusive courses of Steve Nison who introduced the western world to the art of Japanese candlestick as a tool for analysing market trends and investment decisions.

I have been working as a full-time trader and an independent financial analyst since 2007 hence I established Trading with David as a niche investment service with a primary focus on FX markets and commodities. During that time, I collaborated with reputable financial trading services and investment magazines. And from 2012 -2013 I worked as a hedge fund manager for an Italian Bank boutique. In 2018, I began providing market analysis and trading ideas for a major European commodity investment company, and up to this date.

I published several trading and investment books to pass on my knowledge and expertise on how to analyse the financial market correctly and have the odds on your side to become a profitable trader. My approach is based on low-risk investment strategies across all markets to achieve a balanced asset allocation through diversification and risk management.

I am currently working on several other books for those who wish to learn more about certain aspects of trading such as Forex, commodities spread trading, options, and ETFs to name a few. Through my books, I coach independent investors on my personal trading strategies and how to apply them in different market conditions.

You can find out more about my educational library at https://tradingwithdavid.com to develop an extraordinary edge to your trading and investments plan with a deep understanding of the macro environment, along with advanced technical analysis and risk management they are designed to build or improve your trading skillset

Preface

Introduction

~

Have you ever dreamt of trading without stress? With options, this dream can become a reality. Thanks to their flexible nature, options allow for a relaxed approach to trading, making it possible to manage your finances with ease.

Options are extremely versatile financial instruments. Originally created to protect investments, they have evolved to become one of the best ways to manage both your savings and your time. They are ideal for those who wish to integrate trading with other primary activities. Options are particularly suited to traders who do not have much time to dedicate to the markets and want to sleep soundly at night, free from market pressures.

These fantastic instruments offer benefits to those who wish to work with stocks and futures without needing a large trading account, as well as to those who prefer a more speculative approach. Due to their flexibility, options can be tailored to the needs of each trader, just like a custom-made suit.

Options are unique: they allow you to profit from the markets without necessarily predicting the price direction. You can benefit from the mere passage of time or market volatility, making them an excellent choice for a variety of strategies.

However, it is crucial to understand that options are complex instruments and require a professional approach, more so than any other financial instrument. Deep knowledge and continuous learning are essential for successful trading.

Options are also perfect for diversifying trading strategies. If an asset is trending, you can buy or sell it. If it is in a sideways phase, you can use options to exploit the passage of time.

"*Options Relaxing Trading*" is a guide for beginners who want to start exploring the world of options in a simple and clear manner. This book will provide you with a solid foundation upon which to build your options trading activity.

Allow yourself to be captivated by the intriguing world of options. Discover how to trade in a relaxed way while minimising risks.

For any questions, do not hesitate to contact me at info@tradingwithdavid.com.

It will be my pleasure to answer all your queries. Also, visit my website at https://tradingwithdavid.com, where you will find free articles, analyses, mini courses and books.

PART ONE: FEATURES OF OPTIONS

The History of Options

CHAPTER 1

Options and futures are close cousins, but options (as their name implies) come with flexibility. The origin of both products is closely tied to a host of commodities, ranging from olives to tulips, onions to grains.

The very first account of options was mentioned in Aristotle's book named "Politics", published in 332 B.C., where he tells the tale of Thales of Miletus, astronomer, philosopher, and mathematician.

Thales was one of the seven sages of ancient Greece. By observing the stars and weather patterns, Thales predicted a huge olive harvest in the year that follows. Understanding that olive presses would be in high demand following such a huge harvest, he could have obtained an enormous profit if he had owned all of the olive presses in the region. However, he did not have that kind of money.

Instead, Thales thought of a brilliant idea. He used a small amount of money as the deposit to secure the use of all of the olive presses in the region: a Call option with the olive presses as the underlying asset. As Thales expected, the harvest was plentiful, and he sold the rights to use all of these olive presses to people who needed them, turning a big fortune.

In the Middle Ages, some Mediterranean area traders also developed credit contracts that were similar to options, where the seller of the contract agreed to purchase cargo if the ship carrying it did not come in on time for the intended purchaser's needs.

Options then turned up again during the tulip mania of 1636. Tulips imported into Europe from Turkey, and Holland quickly became a symbol of affluence and beauty in the seventeenth century. Due to the overwhelming demand for tulips, demand for tulip bulbs by growers and dealers also increased exponentially, pushing up the price at the producer level.

As the price of tulip bulbs increased almost on a daily basis, Dutch dealers started tulip bulb options trading so that producers could own the rights to own tulip bulbs in advanced and secure a definite buying price.

Even though options trading gained a bad name, it does not stop financiers and investors from acknowledging its speculative power through its inherent leverage. Options were given an organised market towards the end of the seventeenth century in London.

With the lessons learnt from the tulip mania still fresh in mind, trading volume was low as investors still feared the "speculative nature" of options. In fact, there was growing opposition to options trading in London, which ultimately led to options trading being declared illegal in 1733.

Since that year, options trading in London was illegal for more than 100 years until it was declared legal again in 1860. A ban of more than a century due to ignorance and fear. The fates of options and futures ultimately diverged, with futures contracts becoming standardised and regulated in the United States long before options, largely due to the fact that America's agricultural industry demanded something more uniform and regimented.

In 1848, born the Chicago Board of Trade. Located in a rapidly growing city smack in the middle of America's heartland, the CBOT offered a solution to seasonal price risk in the agricultural industry. The CBOT allowed for the trading of "to-arrive" contracts (or "forward" contracts), which allowed farmers to fix a price and delivery date ahead of time, so they could store their product elsewhere until the expected delivery date, centralising what had been a dispersing process.

By 1865, the Board of Trade standardised its contracts transforming the forward contracts marketplace into a standardised futures contract marketplace with uniformity in expiration dates, contract quality and pricing; a product very similar to the futures that you trade today.

In the century that followed, futures grew more uniform and, in the U.S., more regulated. The Grain Futures Act of 1922 created a predecessor to the Commodity Futures Trading Commission, and the first mandatory clearing system to settle trades was established in 1925.

Options, on the other hand, remained unstandardised and largely unregulated in the U.S. and internationally. Options had strong critics due to some of the notable cases where the inability to require counterparties to fulfil their obligations led to big losses on what should have been a profitable position, and in some parts of Europe, they were actually outlawed.

Without a standardised market, each option contract and each term of the contract (strike price, expiration date and cost) had to be individually negotiated. It was not until the late 19th century that New York-based financier Russell Sage put forth a method of pricing options in relation to the price of the underlying security and interest rates, creating a form of standardised pricing.

However, in the early 1900s, fraudulent brokerage houses that peddled speculative or fake securities, popped up across the country, leaving a number of jilted investors in their wake and leaving the options industry unpopular with investors.

The stock market crash of 1929 led to a wide-ranging overhaul of financial regulation. The Securities Act of 1933 created a broad set of regulations governing securities trading while the Securities Exchange Act of 1934 created regulations governing the operation of securities exchanges and created the U.S. Securities and Exchange Commission to enforce the new rules.

The Chicago Board of Trade applied for registration as a national securities exchange shortly after and received a license as such. But that license went unused for more than three decades as the market continued to trade non-standardized privately negotiated options contracts. The Put and Call Brokers and Dealers Association was formed around this same time to organise the over-the-counter markets better.

It was not until the 1960s, in the midst of a grain market crisis, the CBOT finally put its exchange license to use as it looked to expand its business to include options. The resulting spun-off entity, the Chicago Board Options Exchange, established open-outcry trading pits similar to those at its affiliated futures exchange and centralised options clearance and settlement.

In 1973, not only did the CBOE open its doors, but two economists, Fischer Black and Myron Scholes, published an article putting forth a model for calculating the theoretical estimate of an options price over time.

The Black-Scholes model is a mathematical formula used to determine the price of a Call or Put option. It takes into account various factors, including the current price of the underlying asset, the strike price, the time to expiration, the volatility of the underlying asset, and the risk-free interest rate.

With an exchange created and a solid model for pricing, new options contracts were issued subject to standardised terms, such as uniform expiration dates and established "strike" prices, or the price at which the option could be exercised. The market flourished and was subject to regulatory oversight on par with U.S. stock markets, with trades guaranteed by a central clearinghouse, The Options Clearing Corporation.

In 1973, options trading at the CBOE was restricted to Call options, which grant the right to buy shares, in just 16 stocks.

Over time, the listed options market has expanded to additional exchanges and products, including Put options, which grant the right to sell shares and cash-settled index options. They allow investors to manage or hedge portfolio exposure and smooth portfolio returns against indexes like the broad-based S&P 500 and Russell 2000, or narrower indexes like the NASDAQ-100. More recently, the options products have expanded to include weekly options, which expire every Friday, instead of once a month.

In 1982, the listed options market hit a milestone when more than 500,000 contracts were traded in a single day. Options popularity continued to increase, and today it is remarkably easy for any investor to place an options trade.

There is an average of more than 11 million options contracts traded every day on more than 3,000 securities, and the market just continues to grow. And thanks to the vast array of internet resources (like the book you are reading), the general public has a better understanding of options than ever before.

Introduction to Options

Chapter 2

Listed for the first time in 1973 in the United States, **Options** are certainly the ideal for those who do not have much time to devote to the markets or for those looking for a way to make the most of their savings, alongside the trading with options to their work.

An option is a contract between two parties, the buyer and the seller, that gives the buyer the right, but not the obligation, to buy (option "*Call*") or sell (option "*Put*") an underlying asset, by a certain date (*expiration date*), at a pre-set price (*strike price*), by paying a sum of money (*premium*).

From this, **the first important feature** that emerges is that by buying an option, your maximum risk is limited to the premium you pay, regardless of how the underlying asset moves. The underlying asset may be a stock, index, commodity, etc.

Options are financial derivative instruments, which means that their price derives from the market price of another asset named underlying. To take an example from everyday life, bread is a derivative of wheat, the wine of the grape, gasoline of crude oil, etc. A change in the price of the underlying asset (wheat, grape, crude oil) will affect the price of bread, wine, and gasoline.

The relationship between the price of the underlying asset and that of the options is, for those who begin to study these instruments, one of the major obstacles to their full understanding. It is useless to deny that in the options, the complexity of the issues involved is undoubtedly greater than in many other financial instruments.

Options allow for much higher flexibility and adaptability than any other investment strategy. However, it is surprising that in many countries, they have restricted use.

Options can be **American or European style**; in the first case, the exercise of the option can be done at any time before the expiration date on the part of the buyer, while in the European options, the purchaser of the option can exercise it only at the expiration date. You will see this distinction better in Chapter 18.

There are two types of options:

1. **CALL**, the buyer has the right, but not the obligation, to buy an underlying asset at a given price (strike price), by a date to be fixed (expiration date), by paying a sum of money (premium).

Buying a Call option means having a bullish view of the underlying, which means that you believe you can make a profit by reason of the price increase of the underlying asset, as long as it takes place by the expiration date of the option.

2. **PUT**, the buyer has the right, but not the obligation, to sell an underlying asset at a given price (strike price) by a certain date (expiration date), by paying a sum of money (premium).

Buying a Put option, the purchaser has a bearish view of the underlying asset and bears the only risk of losing the invested premium, benefiting from a drop in the price of the underlying asset, provided it takes place by the expiration date of the option.

So, by buying a Call option or a Put option, you are directional on the market.

Another element of options is the premium, that is, the amount of capital the market requires from you to buy an option. You can see an example of an option with Microsoft in Figure 1 below.

MSFT Dec17'21 310 CALL · 5.95 6.05 ·

Figure 1 - Call option on Microsoft (Mexem.com)

MSFT is the ticker of the underlying asset (Microsoft), Dec17'21 is the option expiration date (December 17, 2021), 310 is the strike price, CALL is the option type, and 5.95 and 6.05 are bid and ask (the premium you pay for buy it).

Very important: to facilitate the relationship with the value of the share, the option price refers to a unit quantity of the underlying asset. What is not actually apparent from Figure 1 is the size of the contract, that is, the numerical ratio between an option and the underlying asset. This ratio is standardised and only varies according to the type of underlying asset.

In this case, since these are American shares, each option holds 100 shares of the underlying asset. That is, 1 Microsoft option represents 100 stocks of the company. By purchasing the option at $6.05, you pay a premium of $605 ($6.05 x 100) that give you the right (but not the obligation) on the expiration date to buy 100 Microsoft shares at $310 each.

By buying a Call option, you earn if the price of the underlying asset will rise above the break-even point. By purchasing a Put option, you earn if the price of the underlying asset will fall below the break-even point. Otherwise, you lose, all or in part, the premium paid.

You obtain the break-even point when you buy a Call option by adding the premium paid to the strike price. Below in Figure 2 is an example. I decide to buy a Netflix CALL option with a strike $700, with an expiration date of 17 December 2021. The premium I pay is $14.50. You find the break-even point calculation with all possible situations, depending on the price.

NFLX Dec17'21 700 CALL $ 14.50		
Break-Even Point (BEP) = $ 700 + $ 14.50 = $ 714.50		
Netflix price	Situation	Buy Call
$ 690	Price < Strike	I lose the Premium = $ 1,450
$ 710	Strike < Price < BEP	I lose (BEP - Price) * 100 = $ 450
$ 725	BEP < Price	I earn (Price - BEP) * 100 = $ 1,050

Figure 2 - Netflix buy Call option situations

When you buy a Put option, instead, the break-even point is obtained by subtracting the premium paid from the strike price. In Figure 3 below, the same example with Netflix but this time I decide to buy a Put option with strike $650, expiration date is always 17 December 2021. The premium I pay is $15.30.

NFLX Dec17'21 650 PUT $ 15.30		
Break-Even Point (BEP) = $ 650 - $ 15.30 = $ 634.70		
Netflix price	Situation	Buy Put
$ 670	Price > Strike	I lose the Premium = $ 1,530
$ 645	Strike > Price > BEP	I lose (Price - BEP) * 100 = $ 1,030
$ 610	BEP > Price	I earn (BEP - Price) * 100 = $ 2,470

Figure 3 - Netflix buy Put option situations

When you buy an option, you have a limited risk, which is defined by the premium paid. In the examples in Figures 2 and 3, the $1,450 paid to buy the Call option and the $1,530 paid to buy the Put option represent the highest risk, unlike a stock that can be subject to strong price movements and cause huge losses.

The profits are, instead, potentially unlimited. Well, it is not completely correct; the price, in theory, can rise indefinitely but an underlying asset (stock in this case) cannot have a negative price. Margins required by the broker are however much lower for an option than for buying the underlying asset directly.

Another important aspect is that, while with the shares and some ETF's you get dividends, given that the options are instruments created directly by the markets (and not by the companies), they do not give dividends (dividends which, as you will see shortly, affect, in any case, the prices of options).

Now a question: why are the options purchased so cheap? Why is the premium you pay so low compared to buying shares? Quite simply, because the odds are not on your side. In order to make money when you buy options, you not only have to predict the direction of the market but also how quickly it will reach at least the break-even point. You will see more about this later.

Let's see now, the elements that affect the value of the option premium.

1. **Moneyness** (high impact). That is, the relationship between the strike price of the option chosen and the price of the underlying asset. There are many options for an underlying asset, just as there are many strike prices to choose from.

Selecting an option instead of another, and having the strike price more or less close to the price of the underlying asset, are characteristics that can completely change the overall profile of the investment.

In Figure 4 below, you can see on the right the strike price and on the left the corresponding premium of the Call options on Netflix with an expiration date, 17 December 2021.

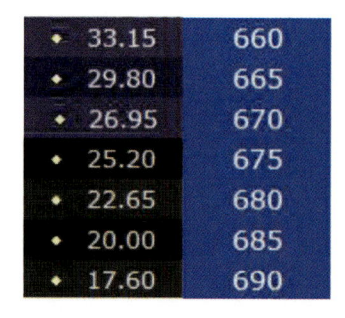

Premium	Strike
33.15	660
29.80	665
26.95	670
25.20	675
22.65	680
20.00	685
17.60	690

Figure 4 - Premium and Strike price of Call option on Netflix (Mexem.com)

You can see that as the strike price changes, so does the premium. This is because the probability of the underlying asset (Netflix) reaching a particular strike price also changes. It will certainly be more likely that Netflix (which currently has a price of $674) will rise to $690 than to $720 or $750 in the next fifty days.

As a rule, the further away an option has a strike price from the price of the underlying asset, the lower the premium will be because the lower the probability that it will have value at the expiration date.

This ratio is quantified by the definitions *in the money* (**ITM**), *at the money* (**ATM**) and *out of the money* (**OTM**). It is very important because it makes you understand what kind of value is reflected in the price depending on the type of option.

CALL options:

a. **ITM (In the Money)**: the price of the underlying asset is less than the strike price.
b. **ATM (At the Money)**: the price of the underlying asset is the same as the strike price.
c. **OTM (Out the Money)**: the price of the underlying asset is less than the strike price.

   PUT options:

a. **ITM (In the Money)**: the price of the underlying asset is less than the strike price.
b. **ATM (At the Money)**: the price of the underlying asset is the same as the strike price.
c. **OTM (Out the Money)**: the price of the underlying asset is more than the strike price.

You can see a practical and visual summary of Disney in Figure 5.

Disney price $ 160		
Strike	CALL	PUT
$ 150	ITM	OTM
$ 155	ITM	OTM
$ 160	ATM	ATM
$ 165	OTM	ITM
$ 170	OTM	ITM

Figure 5 - Disney types of strike price of an option

Depending on the Moneyness, there can be a maximum of two components that, together, form the total price of the options:

a) **Intrinsic Value** exists only in the ITM options and corresponds to the difference between the price of the underlying asset and the strike price (Call options) and between the strike price and the price of the underlying asset (Put options). It can never have a negative value. An example: Disney's price is $160, the intrinsic value of the Call option strike price of $150 is equal to $160 - $150 = $10; the one of the Put option strike price of $180 is: $180 - $160 = $20. The intrinsic value changes only in relation to the change in the price of the underlying asset and not in the passage of time. In practice, the intrinsic value of an option represents its value if it were exercised at that time.

To summarise:

Intrinsic Value Call = Underlying asset price - Strike Call option

Intrinsic Value Put = Strike Put option - Underlying asset price

b) **Extrinsic Value** (or time value) until shortly before the expiration date exists for all three Moneyness and is equal to the difference between the option's price and the possible intrinsic value. You can consider the time value as the additional price that the buyer pays to the seller in order to buy that particular type of option. The OTM option premium is entirely made up of time value, as these options have no intrinsic value. The extrinsic value is linked to factors that do not depend on the performance of the underlying, e.g., the expiration of the option and volatility.

Extrinsic Value = Premium - Extrinsic Value

2. **Expiration** (high impact). Having a well-defined expiration date is one of the features that differentiates options from stocks, bringing them closer, but only for this feature, to futures contracts.

NFLX Nov19'21 700 CALL	7.55
NFLX Dec17'21 700 CALL	15.35
NFLX Jan21'22 700 CALL	28.15
NFLX Feb18'22 700 CALL	35.30
NFLX Mar18'22 700 CALL	39.78

Figure 6 - Netflix different expiration dates and premiums (Mexem.com)

Depending on the expiration date you select, this will affect the premium you have to pay to purchase the option. In Figure 6 above, you can see on the right the premium and on the left the different expiration dates of the Netflix Call option, strike price $700.

The further away is the expiration date, the greater is the time limit for Netflix to arrive at a specific strike price, and the more the premium increases.

It happens because Netflix is much more likely to rise at least to $300 for example, in three months than in only one and, for this reason, we will pay a higher premium for buying the Call option.

As a rule, the furthest the expiration date of an option, and higher the premium of both Call and Put options.

Depending on the type of expiration date, there are 4 different option categories available on the market:

Weekly. They started to be traded on October 28, 2005, with, as an underlying asset, the Standard & Poor 500 (SPX) index, while from June 2010 the weekly options on some ETFs (SPY, QQQ, DIA, IWM) were made available, and then on several stocks.

The main peculiarity of the weekly options is, of course, the duration; in fact, unlike the monthly options, the weekly ones usually are made available at the market opening on Thursdays and expire on the Friday of the following week. Their life cycle is, therefore, only eight days, two of which with the markets closed (Saturday and Sunday). The obligations and requirements are equal to the monthly options.

Given their short life, everything in the weekly options is amplified: the possible profits, as well as the potential losses due to an adverse movement of the underlying asset of the duration even of only a couple of days.

In order to be used in a profitable manner, they, therefore, need great mastery and experience, as well as decidedly greater availability of time than is required by the monthly options.

Monthly. It is the most popular and used type of option and expires typically on the third Friday of the month. The broker automatically provides all the expiration dates currently available.

Quarterly. They have been introduced on the market since 2006 and have the characteristic of expiring at the end of each quarter (i.e., the last working day of March, June, September, and December).

Compared to monthly options, quarterly ones usually have lower liquidity, which is why they can rarely be used in preference to them or considered an equally valid alternative.

Currently, quarterly options are available only for a few underlying assets.

LEAPS (Long-Term Equity Anticipation Security). These are options whose duration is considerably longer than the others: on average nine months, but they can be up to three years.

The LEAPS, introduced on the market in 1990, always expire in January and are mainly used as a valid alternative to the purchase of the underlying asset. Both because they need a decidedly lower capital, and because by having such a long expiration, they limit as much as possible the phenomenon of the time value erosion (time decay that we will see later in the chapter), so characteristic, instead, of the weekly, monthly and quarterly options.

3. Dividend (low impact). The dividend is that part of the net company profit which, after being entered into the balance sheet, is distributed to the shareholders as a return on the invested capital.

Although not standing among the most important factors, the dividend, however, has an impact on the determination of an option's price. Obviously, if the stock or the ETF pays no dividend, or if you are working with futures or commodities, the question of a dividend makes no difference.

What usually happens is: the day the stock will trade ex-dividend, the open will be at a lower price by an amount equal to the dividend itself. The market takes into account this mechanism in the premium of the related options with an expiration date exceeding the coupon date.

In particular, the dividend will lower the premium of a Call option and higher the one of a Put option.

4. Interest rate (very low impact). Of the five factors that can influence the price of an option, the interest rate is the one with the least impact.

In fact, this variation is usually limited to 0.25% (or 25 basis points) and occurs very rarely. I will spare you the reasoning behind it, as it is tedious and, for the purpose of this book, of little interest.

5. Volatility (high impact). The last and most important element that affects the value of an option, is volatility. It can be defined as the measure expressed in percentage points of the speed and extent of changes in the value of a specific asset in a given period of time.

The increase in volatility is mostly reflected in OTM options which in some cases can even double in price with an increase in volatility of only a few percentage points. Each market may have particular and different volatility characteristics, and it may differ significantly depending on the time period analysed.

The options volatility is always referring to the underlying asset and is divided into:

a. Historical volatility is an indicator of the extent to which a price may diverge from its average in a given period. Hence, increased price fluctuation results in a higher historical volatility value. It is, therefore, a certain fact, not subject to opinions or expectations, measurable objectively and totally based on what has already happened.

I will spare you all the calculations and show you an example. Apple stock has a value of $165, and in the last year has had historical volatility of 10%. It means that in the previous 12 months, it has deviated from its average price by $16.5 (10% of $165).

A not very intuitive characteristic of historical volatility is that at high percentage values, not always correspond considerable price differences between the beginning and the end of the period of time are taken into consideration.

b. Implied volatility represents the market's expectations about a likely movement in an underlying asset. It is, therefore, a question of "forecasting", not as in the case of historical volatility, of objective data.

This is the type of volatility that interests you because it is the one that influences the value (premium) of the options. Possible future movements of the underlying asset correspond to increasing values of implied volatility and therefore, higher prices of the corresponding options.

The value of the implied volatility is closely connected, in addition to the strike price, also to the residual life of the option. It may, therefore, happen that options of the same underlying asset but with different expiries have implied volatilities that are also very different.

It is possible to know the value of the implied volatility only for those underlying assets that have the options; otherwise, it is not possible to calculate this type of volatility.

A high value of implied volatility does not necessarily mean that the underlying asset is undergoing large price changes. What affects the implied volatility are future expectations, not the current behaviour of the underlying asset.

It is, therefore, possible to observe an underlying asset with options characterised by high values of implied volatility, but that moves sideways in terms of price.

High values of implied volatility can, therefore, act as a wake-up Call regarding that particular underlying asset. It means that the market expects future large price movements, and this information is very important when you decide to open a trade on that underlying asset.

An increase in implied volatility is usually associated with strong bearish movements, while a growing market is expected to cause a decrease in this type of volatility. In reality, it is not always so. Indeed, the opposite can also happen; it depends on the underlying asset you are using as well.

The elements that affect volatility are:

i. **Earnings**. American companies are required to issue a series of data on the company's performance every three months. Depending on the data, you can witness significant fluctuations, even by several percentage points in a single day.

In proximity to the earnings, volatility begins to grow because the market knows that when earnings are released, the stock could move heavily up or down. For this reason, it is not advisable to buy options before earnings because you would pay a much higher premium (in addition to the fact that earnings can also be very negative for your position).

ii. **Rumours**. Another element that can alter the price of an underlying asset is "rumours." Rumours of acquisitions, capital increases, etc., even though not confirmed, create nervousness in the markets, thus increasing volatility.

iii. **Panic Selling**. Following corporate actions or economic and political events, particularly serious and important, it can follow strong sales by all investors, causing panic selling, and resulting in a sharp increase in volatility.

Just think about what happened after September 11 or the Volkswagen stock on 19 September 2015, the day after the news of the scandal of the diesel emission data in the United States (-18.60%). In either case, volatility went through the roof.

Other factors that cause increased volatility are macroeconomic data, central bank meetings and interest rate decisions, tensions between major oil-producing countries, terrorist attacks, and all that can cause nervousness and uncertainty in financial markets.

You have seen that buying an option can be very beneficial because it gives you the opportunity to buy or sell an underlying asset at a better price than the market price. If you are good at finding where an underlying can go, with the options, you will have a chance to earn far more than not working directly on the underlying asset.

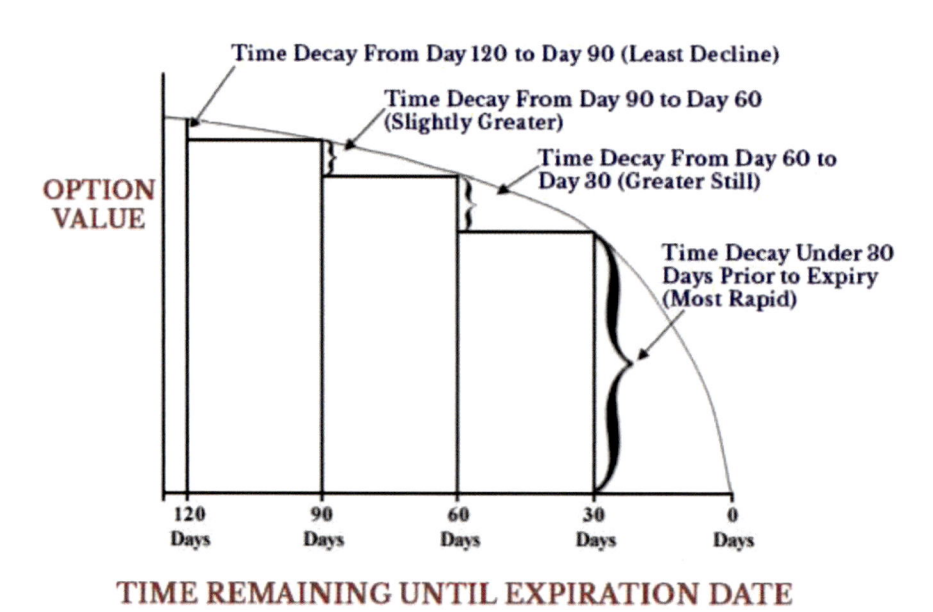

Figure 7 - Time Decay in an option

By buying options, however, you have not only positive aspects but several elements that play against you. The first of these elements is time. When you buy options, time is not your friend because every passing day your option loses a bit of value. You can see the time decay of an option in Figure 7 above.

Time decay, therefore, is the phenomenon for which, with the passage of time, the option loses value. This is because the closer you get to the expiration date and less time there is for the option to reach at least the break-even point.

The residual maturity of an option has a significant impact on its price, in particular for the at-the-money (ATM) and out-the-money (OTM) options.

Important. The options that lose the most in value are the ATM options, but those that lose the most in percentage are the OTM options. So, the OTM options are the ones that lose value faster with the passage of time, as you can see in the chart in Figure 8.

To indicate the time value is used a Greek called Theta. When you see this symbol θ (Theta) on your trading platform, its value tells you how much an option depreciates with the passage of time. In Appendix B, you can find an exhaustive explanation of the main Greeks.

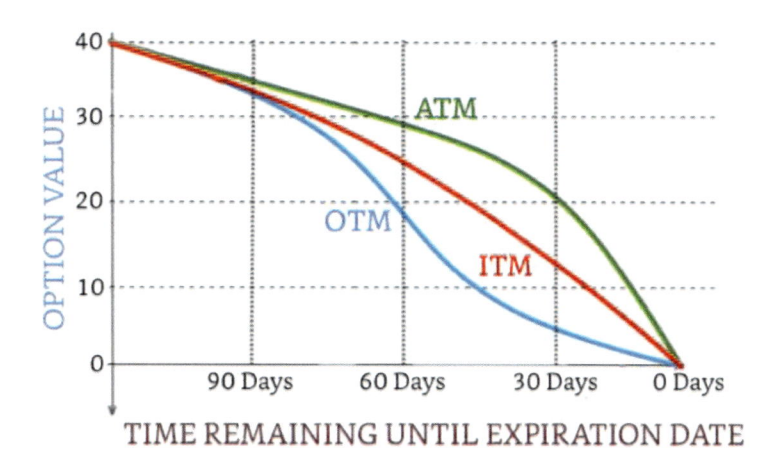

Figure 8 - Moneyness Time Decay

    The probability is a second element that plays against you in buying options. If you buy a Call option, you will only earn if the underlying rises and even with strength. If it goes down, moves sideways, or rises but not enough to reach at least the break-even point, you will lose the premium paid (or part of it).

    The same if you buy a Put option, you will only gain if the price of the underlying asset will fall below the break-even point. Our odds of success are, therefore, 1:4, which is 25%.

    Clarification. You are not forced to hold a purchased option until the expiration date. You can resell it when you find it more appropriate, as you can see in the example below.

    Facebook has a price of $316, and I decide to buy a Call option, with a strike price of $320, and an expiration date of December 17, 2021 (about two months) because I expect the stock price to go up. The premium is $12.90, so I pay the option purchase at $1,290. After two weeks, Facebook has risen to $320, and for the same option I bought, the premium is now $18.50.

    I can choose to keep the option in my portfolio for a little longer because I expect Facebook to increase in value again. Or I can decide to sell it and collect a premium of $1,750, for a net profit of $560 (the $1,850 I got by selling the option minus the $1,290 I paid to buy it).

    You have therefore seen that if you buy an option, in the face of a small premium paid, you can make a significant profit; nevertheless, time and odds are not on your side.

    It does not mean that buying options is wrong, absolutely not. The purchase of options, however, is difficult to earn because this requires a lot of precision in identifying where an underlying asset will move and by a precise date. And, above all, it does not allow you to earn steadily over time: month after month, year after year.

    As an options trader, you can be either the buyer or the seller, exactly like with any other financial instrument. In the next chapter, you will discover the true essence of options, what makes them the financial instrument with the greatest likelihood of success.

Selling Options

CHAPTER 3

~

You have seen that buying options can be very beneficial because it allows you to buy or sell an underlying asset at an advantageous price, with very low risk and limited to the premium you paid to buy the option. You also saw that there are some negative sides, the time it is against you, and the odds of success are low. But there is another essential element to be taken into account: the quality of life.

An important and underestimated thing in trading is that it does not matter how much you earn, but how you do it. Much better to earn a little less but sleep soundly rather than gain more but with high stress.

Buying options means you have to stand in front of a monitor to follow the position, with much less time to dedicate to the family, your own interests, and so on. This does not happen when you sell an option and this is a top priority for me. When you sell an option, everything you have seen in the previous chapter is reversed. You no longer have to predict how a market (underlying asset) will move by a certain date (expiration date), but where you think it will not.

By reformulating the definition (this time from the point of view of the seller), an option is a contract between two parties, the buyer and the seller, that gives the seller the obligation, to sell (option "*Call*") or buy (option "*Put*") an underlying asset, by a date to be fixed (*expiration date*), at a pre-set price (*strike price*), by collecting a sum of money (*premium*).

From this, **the first important feature** that emerges is that, unlike when you buy options, when you sell options, your maximum risk is unlimited.

Now, therefore, you no longer have a right, but an obligation that is to sell (Call option) or buy (Put option) the underlying asset at the strike price, if the option is in the money at expiration and you will be assigned. You will see more about the assignment in Chapter 18.

Let's see again the two types of options, this time not on the side of the buyer, but from the seller's perspective.

1. **CALL**. The selling of a Call option gives you the obligation to sell the underlying at a fixed price (strike price), by a certain date (expiration date), by collecting a sum of money

(premium). Selling a Call option presupposes a sideways or bearish view of the underlying asset, so you are not bullish.

2. **PUT**. The selling of a Put option gives you the obligation to buy the underlying at a fixed price (strike price), by a certain date (expiration date), and by collecting a sum of money (premium). Selling a Put option presupposes a sideways or bullish view of the underlying asset, so you are not bearish.

Thus, with the sale of options, the seller, unlike the buyer, no longer has a right but is in the position of having an obligation to the counterparty.

Now, the premium no longer represents your maximum risk but your maximum (potential) gain. The maximum profit (premium) can only be obtained in full at the expiration of the option if it will not be profitable for the buyer to exercise the option (so that the premium will remain entirely in the seller's pocket). In this case, the option is said to expire worthless.

By selling a Call option, you earn if the price of the underlying asset will close below the break-even point. You obtain the break-even point by adding the premium collected to the strike price. Figure 9 is an example. I decide to sell a Facebook CALL option with a strike of $350, and an expiration date of 17 December 2021. The premium I collect is $4.55. Here is the break-even point calculation with all possible situations, depending on the price.

FB Dec17'21 350 CALL $ 4.55		
Break-Even Point (BEP) = $ 350 + $ 4.55 = $ 354.55		
Facebook price	Situation	Sell Call
$ 340	Price < Strike	I earn the Premium = $ 455
$ 352	Strike < Price < BEP	I earn (BEP - Price) * 100 = $ 255
$ 360	BEP < Price	I lose (Price - BEP) * 100 = $ 545

Figure 9 - Facebook sell Call option situations

In Figure 10, you can see the same example with Facebook but this time I decide to sell a Put option with strike $290, expiration date is always 17 December 2021. The premium I collect is $5.10.

FB Dec17'21 290 PUT $ 5.10		
Break-Even Point (BEP) = $ 290 - $ 5.10 = $ 284.90		
Facebook price	Situation	Sell Put
$ 310	Price > Strike	I earn the Premium = $ 510
$ 287	Strike > Price > BEP	I earn (Price - BEP) * 100 = $ 210
$ 275	BEP > Price	I lose (BEP - Price) * 100 = $ 890

Figure 10 - Facebook sell Put option situations

The elements that affect the premium are the same as you saw in the previous chapter (moneyness, expiration, volatility, etc.), but from a different point of view. While with the buying of options you have to try to obtain a premium as low as possible, by having to pay, with the selling you have to try to get a premium that is as high as possible, because, this time, you collect it.

In a low volatility period, unlike when you buy options, it is less convenient to sell them because also the premiums are low. But it should also be said that low volatility indicates markets little nervous and therefore with fewer sudden movements.

An important indicator of volatility and "measure" of market nervousness is the VIX (also called the "Fear Index"). Vix is based on the prices of options on the S&P 500 Index and is calculated by aggregating weighted prices of the index's Call and Put options over a wide range of strike prices. It is a good indicator of the expectation of market volatility (implied volatility).

Below in Figure 11, you can see the VIX chart (in blue) compared to the S&P 500 index (in black). You can easily see how the two indexes are inversely correlated. If the S&P 500 index increases, the VIX decreases and vice versa, if the index falls, the VIX rises.

Figure 11 - VIX and S&P500 chart (TradingView.com)

You will see in Chapter 17 how to use the VIX in your trades to cover you from any volatility swings.

The selling of options also reversed the negative aspects you saw with the purchase. Now, time and probability are on your side. Time in the selling of options is your precious ally. Now, in fact, time decay is a big friend. With each passing day, the option you sold will lose a bit of its value, especially, as you have seen in the previous chapter, over the past 30 days.

Now, you will no longer have the frenzy that the underlying asset moves forcefully and rapidly in your direction, as when you buy an option. A simple sideways movement of the underlying asset (with a consequent reduction in volatility) is enough to see the written option lose value. The probability of obtaining a profit by selling the options is very high. As you have seen, when you buy an option, you are directional with the underlying asset; basically, you will have a 25% chance of bringing home a profit.

When you sell an option, you are, instead, non-directional with the underlying asset. When you sell, for example, a Call option, you will get a profit if the underlying asset falls, moves sideways, or rises but not enough to reach the strike price sold. Your odds of success, then, rise up to 75%.

In selling the options, it is all a lot simpler, starting with the fact that you already know your maximum gain (the premium). You do not have to stress yourself about how to handle the operation, frustrated between the lines of "*I should close*" and "*it is better to keep the position open a little longer*" (here we come back to the concept of a better quality of life).

For the same reason, however, the elements that, with the purchase of options are on your side, are now against you. While when you buy an option, your risk is limited to the premium paid, and for that, the broker asks you for a low margin, now, your risk is, without due precautions, potentially unlimited and the margin the broker asks is much higher. This is because the margin required by the broker reflects the risk of the trade; the riskier the trade, the higher the margin required.

I conclude with an example. After your analysis, you are sure that in the coming weeks, Goldman Sachs will not rise above $450 (current price $425). You, therefore, decide to sell the Call option with an expiration date, of 17 December 2021, a strike price of $450, and a premium of $5.50 (that is, $550).

To sell the option, the broker asks you for a margin of $14,000. So, to get a profit of $500, you use a capital (margin) of $14,000, with the risk of losing much more.

Why, then, should the seller take such a big risk for a limited profit? If you are asking yourself this question, you have forgotten one important thing: the odds of success, which in the selling of options are 75% (and that with simple but profitable strategies, can rise to 85/90%).

And for the remaining 10/15%? In Chapter 6, you will see how to limit the loss. For the moment, you finish seeing the characteristics of the options with the next two chapters.

Options vs Stocks

Chapter 4

Is it better to buy stock or a Call option? I will start by saying that both instruments are valid; it depends on how you intend to use them and what your objective is. You have already seen that an option is different from a stock. A stock is a share of ownership in a company that decides to list on the stock exchange. Companies issue stocks to raise capital to invest and thus avoid borrowing from banks. Options, on the other hand, are derivative instruments created directly by the markets. For this reason, stocks pay dividends; options do not.

A characteristic of options is that they are subject to expiration. Unlike stocks, which are listed throughout the year, options have an expiration date that can range from a few days to several years. However, by purchasing an option, you have lower risk, with a loss limited to the premium paid. This means that the broker will require a lower margin compared to buying 100 shares, which can also generate significant losses.

To better understand, let me give you a practical example. I decide to buy 100 Microsoft shares at a price of $325 for an investment of $32,500. The margin required to open the operation (which can vary depending on the broker) is $8,125. If Microsoft rises, for example, to $340, I gain (($340 - $325) x 100 = $1,500). If it falls, for example, to $300, I lose (($325 - $300) x 100 = $2,500). Buying and selling shares makes it very easy to understand at any moment what the potential profit or loss is.

As for the maximum loss I can incur, this is represented by the capital invested in the case of stock purchase (in my example $32,500). But if I decided to buy options on Microsoft, what risks would I face?

First of all, since it is an American stock, 1 option represents 100 shares, so it is sufficient to buy just one option to open a position of the same size as the one in stocks described above. Then, I have to decide on the strike price and the expiration date. If the strike price choice is simple, I would choose the ATM option ($325) to invest the same capital used in buying 100 shares; for the expiration date, we go back to the beginning of the chapter: it depends on the objective of my investment.

If my operation has a short-term vision (at most a few weeks) with the aim of taking advantage of a bullish movement of the stock, I will choose an expiration date of one or two months. If instead, the operation is broader, I will decide on a more distant expiration date so that the time decay will not affect the price of the options much, at least for the first few months.

I decide to buy the MSFT Dec17'21 325 Call option (with expiration in 50 days) which has a price of $8.50. So, by paying a premium of $850, I gain (and lose) as if I had invested $32,500. Leaving aside the correctness of my analysis, let's see practically what the differences are between the two types of investment. In both cases, I invest $32,500. While with shares the broker requires a margin of $8,125, with the option this is reduced to $850 (note that this margin varies depending on the chosen expiration date). [Therefore, by buying the option, I have an advantage]().

While the maximum gain is the same for the two types of activity (theoretically unlimited), the loss is not. With shares, I have a maximum potential loss of the entire capital invested, $32,500 (if the price of Microsoft drops to zero). With the option, my maximum loss is limited to the premium paid, $850. [Here too, with the option, I have an advantage]().

However, it is necessary to make a distinction. While in the purchase of shares, the only cost consists of commission fees, with the option I also have the premium paid. If, for example, at the expiration date, the price of Microsoft is $330, with shares I would obtain a gain of $500 minus the commission fees; with the option, I would incur a certain loss of $850 (premium paid), plus commission fees, minus $500 (Microsoft gain). Therefore, the premium I pay is a non-refundable cost. [Here, with the option, I have a disadvantage]().

Of course, the problem does not exist if I decide not to exercise the option at the expiration date, but to sell it earlier. In this case, other dynamics related to the premium come into play.

Two variables influence options, while shares are indifferent to them: volatility and time. By buying the option, volatility can give you an advantage or a disadvantage. First of all, it influences the price of the option, so when you decide to buy the option, the premium you pay will also depend on the implied volatility at the time. With low volatility, you will pay a lower premium; with high volatility, it will be more expensive to buy the option.

So, it is true that the margin required by the broker is lower if I buy the option, however, it can grow in periods of high volatility (and I cannot wait for it to decrease, the price of Microsoft will not wait for me). This translates into a farther break-even point (therefore lower profit if I decide to hold the option until the expiration date) and a higher maximum loss. [In this case, with the option, I might have a disadvantage]().

Volatility can also be a favourable factor. If Microsoft moves sideways, with shares I will practically not gain, while if the implied volatility increases, even if Microsoft is not in an upward trend, my option will gain the same. Here, with the option, I might have an advantage.

Additionally, a spike in volatility (acceleration) can lead the option to gain or lose a much higher percentage than shares. You will see this better in Chapter 20. So, with the option, I can have an advantage but also a disadvantage.

Finally, time, which as you have seen, takes away some value from the option with each passing day, while it has no effect on shares. Buying the option, I have a disadvantage. Therefore, it is important, as already mentioned, to choose the correct expiration date, based on your goal and strategy.

In the following scheme, you can read a summary of the pros and cons of the two financial instruments, shares and options:

Stocks

Pros: Dividends.
They are not subject to expiration.
Cons: Potentially limitless risk.
They are expensive (high margin).

Options

Pros: They are cheap (low margin).
Very high risk/reward ratio.
Limited risk.
Cons: No dividends.
They are subject to expiration.
Lower profit probabilities (time).

What you have seen is valid for both buying Call and Put options, while it changes completely for selling options, but here it is not possible to make a comparison with shares. You will get a better look at selling options in the second part of the book.

In the next chapter, you will finish seeing the characteristics of options by understanding the two different uses they can have, the speculative one you have seen so far and the hedging one.

HEDGING OR SPECULATION

CHAPTER 5

~

You have seen what options are, their characteristics, their strengths, and weaknesses, but you have only seen one way to use them, the speculative one. That is, exploiting an increase (buying) or a decrease (selling) in the premium to take home a profit.

However, options, by their nature, are originally intended for another purpose: to provide coverage for those directly or indirectly connected to an underlying asset. I will give you some examples to better understand this type of use, but I must tell you right away that traders mostly use options for speculative purposes.

The first example concerns stocks. You have bought 100 Apple shares at $165 each, but the US stock market is at its peak, and you fear a reversal or at least a retracement. However, you want to keep the shares in your portfolio. How can you protect your investment? There are two main ways: using a Covered Call strategy (you will see the strategy in more detail in Chapter 14) or buying a Put option.

First strategy: Covered Call

This is the current situation:

- Purchase price of Apple shares: $165;
- Number of shares owned: 100.

Here are the actions to take:

- Sell a Call option with a strike price of $200 and a 30-day expiry;
- For selling the Call option, you collect a premium of $2 (a total of $200).

Let's see all the possible scenarios:

1. If the price of Apple rises above $200, your shares will be sold at $200 each.

Gain = (Sale Price - Purchase Price) x Number of Shares + Premium Collected

So:

($200 - $165) x 100 + $200 = $3,700

2. If the price of Apple shares remains below $200 but above $165 until the option expiry, the option will expire worthless, and you will keep both the shares (which will have a value at least equal to the initial price) and the premium.
3. If the price of Apple falls below $165, the $200 premium collected covers part of the loss. More precisely, you are covered up to:

Purchase Price of the Share - Premium Collected

So

$165 - $2 = $163

If the price of Apple falls below $163, you will incur a loss.

However, this strategy has limitations.

- If the price of Apple rises significantly above $200, the gain is limited to $200 per share.
- If the price falls, the premium collected may not fully cover the losses.

Second strategy: buying a Put option

Buying a Put option gives you the right to sell the shares at a specific price by a certain date, protecting your investment against a drop in the share price. The initial situation is always the same.

- Purchase price of Apple shares: $165;
- Number of shares owned: 100.

Here are the actions to take.

- Buy a Put option with a strike price of $165 and a 30-day expiry;
- For buying the Put option, you pay a premium of $3 (a total of $300).

Let's now see all the possible scenarios.

1. If the price of Apple rises or remains above $165, the Put option will expire worthless, and the loss is limited to the premium paid for the option.

Total loss = Premium paid for the option = $300

2. If the price of Apple falls below $165, you can exercise the option and sell the shares at $165. Again, the loss is limited to the premium paid for the option.

Total loss = Premium paid for the option = $300

However, also this strategy has limitations.

- The cost of the Put option premium slightly reduces the potential net gain.
- If the price rises, the Put option premium is a lost expense, but this is common for any type of insurance, such as car insurance.

Using a Covered Call strategy or buying a Put option are two effective methods to protect your stock portfolio. The choice between the two depends on your type of investment, market forecast, time perspective, protection duration, risk tolerance, and financial goal. The Covered Call generates additional income and offers limited protection, while buying a Put option offers more comprehensive protection against losses at an additional cost.

Depending on your strategy and stop-loss, you can use a Vertical Spread (you will see the Vertical Spread in the second part), like a Bull Put, to pay less for your "insurance".

Using options for coverage is not only useful for those who speculate on financial markets to protect their portfolio. Have you ever wondered how large companies can guarantee themselves a profit margin?

Let me explain with another example. A refinery needs to buy crude oil and transform it into derivative products like gasoline and diesel. Currently, the price of crude oil is $82 per barrel. The refinery cannot afford a price higher than $95; otherwise, its profit margin would disappear. To protect itself from a potential price increase, the refinery can buy a Call option.

Operation specifications:

- Current price of crude oil: $82 per barrel;
- Maximum tolerable price (strike price): $95 per barrel;
- Option duration: 6 months;
- Call option premium: $2 per barrel;
- Refinery consumption: 1000 barrels every six months.

Before proceeding, a couple of clarifications are necessary. Unlike stocks, with commodities, an option represents not 100 but 1 futures contract. In this case, an option represents a futures contract on crude oil which, in turn, has a size of 1000 barrels.

Also, to simplify things, let's say the refinery has a consumption of 1000 barrels of crude oil every six months. This way, it needs to buy only one Call option to hedge. Let's proceed.

Option details:

- Type of option: Call;
- Strike price: $95;
- Expiry date: six months;
- Premium paid: $2 per barrel.

The refinery pays a premium of $2 per barrel, which covers 1000 barrels, so a total of $2000. This premium guarantees the refinery the right to buy crude oil at a maximum price of $95 per barrel in six months. The maximum cost for the refinery will therefore be:

Maximum cost = Strike price of the purchased option + Premium paid

That is:

Maximum cost = $95 + $2 = $97 (per barrel)

By doing so, the refinery risks paying for the oil in six months much more than its current cost, that is, $82 per barrel. The problem is that companies do not always have the necessary liquidity for supplies and thus need to resort to derivatives like options to stabilize their accounts and not be at the mercy of the typical ups and downs of a commodity like crude oil, whose price fluctuations are not only due to economic factors but also often unpredictable geopolitical situations.

Let's now see the possible scenarios.

The price of crude oil drops to $65

- Market price: $65 per barrel;
- Total cost for the refinery: $65 (market price) + $2 (premium) = $67 per barrel;
- Refinery action: the refinery does not exercise the Call option because it can buy crude oil at a lower price in the market;
- Conclusion: the refinery is happy to lose the $2 premium because the total cost is significantly lower than what it would have paid by exercising the option ($67 vs. $95).

The price of crude oil rises to $110

- Market price: $110 per barrel;
- Total cost for the refinery: $95 (strike price) + $2 (premium) = $97 per barrel;
- Refinery action: the refinery exercises the Call option to buy crude oil at $95 per barrel, avoiding paying the higher market price;
- Conclusion: the refinery saves $13 per barrel compared to the market price ($110 - $97 = $13), protecting its profit margin.

Let's now see the advantages of hedging with options.

- Cost stability: the refinery can plan costs with greater certainty, reducing uncertainty related to crude oil price fluctuations.
- Risk protection: the refinery is protected from unexpected price increases that could compromise the profit margin.
- Flexibility: if prices fall, the refinery can benefit from lower market prices, losing only the premium paid for the option.

Companies, like refineries, use derivatives like options to stabilize their accounts and manage the risks associated with commodity price fluctuations. These fluctuations depend not only on economic factors but also on often unpredictable geopolitical situations. Using options allows companies to focus on their core business without worrying excessively about the price variations of basic materials.

Now let's look at the other side of the coin. Oil companies, like other major producers, use options to protect their profit margins against commodity price fluctuations. I will show you, through an example, two different strategies depending on the situation, then analysing the advantages and disadvantages of each.

Here is the example. Let's take an oil company with an extraction cost of $70 per barrel that wants to ensure it sells the extracted crude oil in the coming months at a minimum price of $85 per barrel.

Strategy 1: Buying a Put option

These are the operation details.

- Extraction price: $70 per barrel;
- Minimum desired selling price: $85 per barrel;
- Strike price of the Put option: $95;
- Put option premium: $10 per barrel;
- Option expiry: 6 months.

By buying a Put option with a strike price of $95 and paying a premium of $10, the company reserves the right to sell oil at $95 per barrel in six months.

Here are all the possible scenarios after six months.

1. The price of crude oil drops to $60

- Market price: $60 per barrel;
- Company action: exercises the Put option;
- Net selling price: $95 (strike price) - $10 (premium paid) = $85 per barrel;
- Conclusion: the company manages to sell the oil at $85 per barrel, guaranteeing the minimum desired price.

2. The price of crude oil rises to $110

- Market price: $110 per barrel;
- Company action: does not exercise the Put option;
- Net selling price: $110 (market price) - $10 (premium paid) = $100 per barrel;
- Conclusion: the company sells the oil at $100 per barrel, benefiting from the market price increase, net of the premium paid.

Strategy 2: Selling a Call option

Operation details:

- Extraction price: $70 per barrel;
- Minimum desired selling price: $85 per barrel;

- Strike price of the Call option: $95;
- Call option premium: $4 per barrel;
- Option expiry: 6 months.

By selling a Call option with a strike price of $95, the company collects a premium of $4 per barrel with the possibility of selling the oil at $95 per barrel in six months.

Let's see all the possible scenarios.

1. The price of crude oil drops to $60

- Market price: $60 per barrel;
- Company action: does not exercise the Call option;
- Net selling price: $60 (market price) + $4 (premium collected) = $64 per barrel;
- Conclusion: the company sells the oil at $64 per barrel, incurring a loss compared to the extraction cost but mitigated by the premium collected.

2. The price of crude oil rises to $110

- Market price: $110 per barrel;
- Company action: is obliged to sell the oil at $95 (strike price);
- Net selling price: $95 (strike price) + $4 (premium collected) = $99 per barrel;
- Conclusion: the company sells the oil at $99 per barrel, earning less than the market price but still benefiting from the premium collected.

3. The price of crude oil is at $90

- Market price: $90 per barrel;
- Company action: does not exercise the Call option;
- Net selling price: $90 (market price) + $4 (premium collected) = $94 per barrel;
- Conclusion: the company sells the oil at $94 per barrel, benefiting from the premium collected and obtaining a better selling price compared to the Put option strategy.

Here are the advantages and disadvantages of the two strategies.

Buying a Put option

Advantages:

- Guarantees a minimum selling price, protecting against significant price drops;
- If the market price rises, the company can still benefit from the increase, net of the premium paid.

Disadvantages:

- Involves a cost (premium) that reduces the net gain;

- If the price remains stable or increases slightly, the Put option might not be necessary.

Selling a Call option

Advantages:

- Collects a premium that increases the net gain;
- Benefits from an improved selling price if the market price remains within a certain range.

Disadvantages:

- Does not guarantee a minimum selling price;
- The company is obliged to sell at the strike price if the market price exceeds this value, losing potential high gains.

The choice between buying a Put option and selling a Call option depends on market prospects, risk management strategies, and the financial needs of the oil company. Buying a Put option offers more secure protection against significant price drops, while selling a Call option can increase gains in a stable or moderately variable price scenario. Both strategies have their pros and cons and can be used complementarily depending on market conditions and business goals.

To conclude, for a trader buying or selling a commodity option like crude oil, the broker generally does not allow physical delivery of the underlying (I recommend checking to avoid unpleasant surprises), but only cash settlement.

The first part of the book ends here. Now you have an idea of what options are and how they are used. In the second part, you will see the first strategy: the Vertical Spread.

PART TWO: VERTICAL SPREAD

Hedging Against the Risk

CHAPTER 6

~

A statistic published by the Chicago Board Options Exchange (CBOE) says that only 10% of options contracts are exercised. However, just because only 10% are exercised does not mean that the other 90% expire worthless. The same statistic says that between 55% and 60% of option contracts are closed before the expiration date. Thus, only 30-35% of contracts certainly expire worthless.

I think it is not too far from the truth when I say that at least 75-80% of option contracts expire worthless. And that is why it is better to be an option seller than a buyer. You have seen that selling options is also advantageous from the point of view of time and probability, but it has potentially unlimited risks. You can lose much more than the money you invested. Let me show you this with an example. I will use SPY, the S&P500 index ETF, you can see the chart in Figure 12.

Figure 12 - Spy daily chart (TradingView)

As you can see, the ETF is in a bullish trend. Every month/month and a half there is a rebound with the index then resuming its climb and reaching new highs.

Now, I do not know what the ETF will do in the coming weeks, whether it will go up further, move sideways or go down. But my guess is that it will not reach 480 in a month's time. This is because the S&P 500 has gone up a lot because it is normal for the market to bounce a little bit and a million other reasons that you can find in an analysis.

So, my strategy is to sell a Call option strike 480, a simple sale of a "naked" option. That way, if at expiry SPY is at or below 480, I collect a premium. But what happens if the market continues to rise? If it has a strong bullish movement?

When I sell naked options, I have certain gains but potentially unlimited risks. And that goes against my idea of trading and what should be yours.

The message I try to get across in my books is not exacerbated or exaggerated speculation, I am not interested in doubling my account every year if it means I cannot sleep at night. Because I can assure you that whatever you can gain if it alters your daily life balance, it is absolutely not worth it. This is the basis of my trading, not just in options.

So how can I get around this problem?

I could protect my trade by placing a stop-loss. For example, I sell a Put option on Netflix with a $5 premium (meaning I collect $500). I can place a stop-loss on the option at $10 or $15 or $20... where I think is the right level.

Placing a stop-loss, however, may not be enough. It may happen that the next day the opening price of the underlying asset is above (gap up) or below (gap down) my stop-loss, or that there is a strong movement of 10% or 15% against my position. The stop-loss is missed and I am unable to close the trade, causing a heavy loss.

Many people think that stop-loss is something automatic and should always work, but it does not. Being influenced by news, central bank decisions, political events, and so on, an underlying asset can make a strong move and the price will jump a stop-loss, causing heavy losses.

Just think back to January 2015 when the Swiss Central Bank released the Swiss franc from its fixed exchange rate of 1.20 against the euro. Everyone who was bullish at that time on the currency pair (but also on the CHF against the other major currencies) suffered heavy losses because all stop-losses were missed.

Several brokers also suffered heavy losses, some of them were forced to declare bankruptcy (like Alpari) or risked having to do so (like FXCM). So how can I prevent this from happening?

There is a way that I will show you in the next chapter.

Vertical Spread

CHAPTER 7

So far you have seen that selling an option is the best way to work. The odds of success are on your side but, unfortunately, the risk is potentially unlimited. At the end of the previous chapter, I mentioned a way to limit your loss when selling an option. I will explain this way with an example.

I decide to sell a Call option on Microsoft, strike price $330 and expiration date 21 January 2022. By selling the option, I collect a premium of $3.50. But I do not stop here. At the same time, I buy a Call option, also on Microsoft, with the same expiration date, but with strike price $335 (slightly more OTM than the option I sold) for which I pay a premium of $2.70. Therefore, the net premium I collect is $3.50 - $2.70 = $0.80 (i.e., $80).

Well, what I have constructed has a name and it is a very specific strategy: Vertical Spread. A Vertical Spread consists of selling an OTM option and buying an even more OTM option with the same expiration date.

With this strategy, you have limited the maximum loss which will be given by:

Max Loss = (high strike - low strike) - premium collected) x 100

For the Microsoft example, the maximum loss (risk) is given by:

Max Loss = ($335 - $330) - $0.80) x 100 = $420

When selling a Vertical Spread constructed with Put options, the maximum loss is always calculated in the same way.

As a rule. From the difference between the two strike prices multiplied by 100, you subtract the net premium collected and you get the maximum loss which is also the risk of the trade.

As you have seen, using this strategy, I sell an option, and for a slightly lower premium due to the premium paid for the purchase of another option, I get a limited maximum loss, and now this aspect does not scare me as much as before.

Vertical spreads can be of two types, depending on whether you want to sell a Call option or a Put option:

1. Bear Call. It consists of selling an OTM Call option and buying another Call option which is even more OTM. In this case, you are not bullish.

Let me show you another example of a Bear Call. I decide to sell a Call option on Apple, strike $160 and buy a Call option on Apple, strike $165. The expiration date is January 21, 2022. I collect a premium on the written option of $2.20 and pay a premium on the purchased option of $1.35. Therefore, the net premium I collect is $2.20 - $1.35 = $0.85 ($85).

The performance of a Vertical Spread, and of any other strategy, can be represented with a graph. In the case of the Bear Call, the performance is as follows (Figure 13):

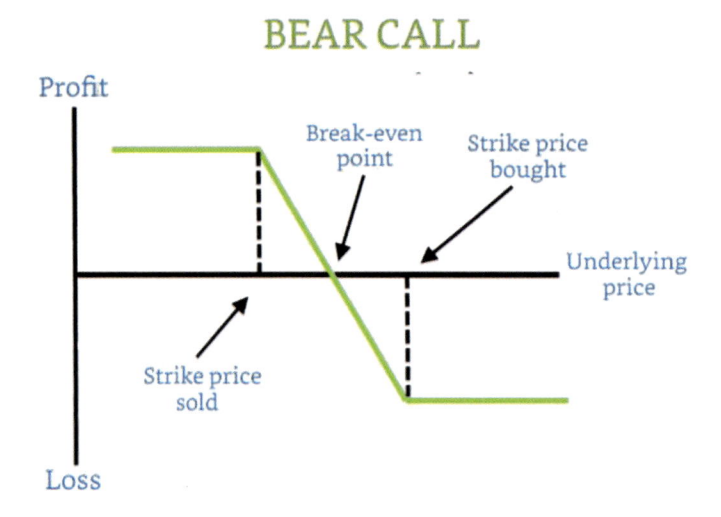

Figure 13 - Performance graph Bear Call

The performance graph is nothing more than a common Cartesian chart with the P&L (Profit & Loss) on the vertical (y) axis and the price of the underlying asset on the horizontal (x) axis.

The maximum loss will occur when the price of the underlying asset is equal to or greater than the strike price of the option purchased (on the right-hand side of the graph). The maximum loss is calculated as follows:

Maximum Loss = ((strike option bought - strike option sold) – premium) x 100

In the example with Apple:

Maximum Loss = ($165 - $160) - $0.85) x 100 = $415

The maximum profit, on the other hand, will be reached when the price of the underlying asset is equal to the strike price of the option sold or lower (on the left-hand side of the graph). The maximum loss is calculated as follows:

Maximum Profit = premium collected

In the example:

Maximum Profit = $85

The breakeven point is the price of the underlying asset at which your trade neither gains nor loses money. When you sell a Bear Call the breakeven point is calculated as follows:

Break-even Bear Call = Strike sold Call option + premium collected

In the example:

Break-even Bear Call = $160 + $0.85 = $160.85

2. **Bull Put**. It consists of selling an OTM Put option and buying another Put option which is even more OTM. In this case, you are not bearish.

Let me show you an example of a Bull Put. I decide to sell a Put option on Facebook, strike $300, and buy a Call option on Facebook, strike $295. The expiration date is February 18, 2022. I collect a premium on the written option of $13.50 and pay a premium on the purchased option of $12.00. Therefore, the net premium I collect is $13.50 - $12.00 = $1.50 ($150). When you sell a Bull Put, the performance is as follows (Figure 14):

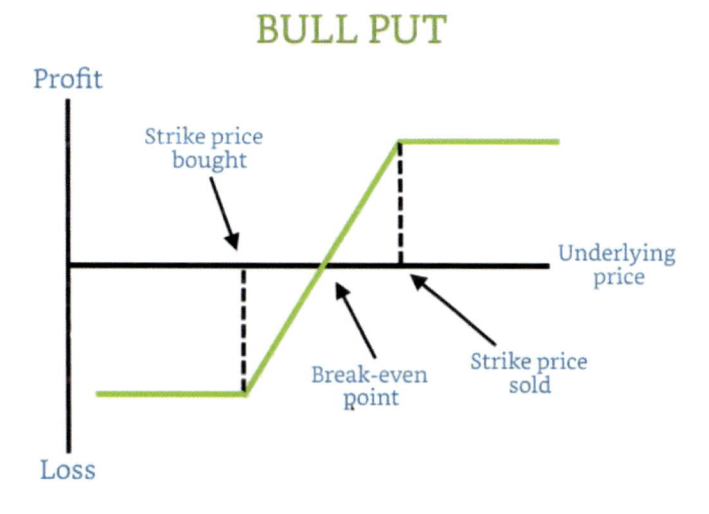

Figure 14 - Performance graph Bull Put

The maximum loss will occur when the price of the underlying asset is equal to the strike price of the option purchased or lower (on the left-hand side of the graph). The maximum loss is calculated as follows:

Maximum Loss = ((strike option sold - strike option bought) - premium) x 100

In the example with Facebook:

Maximum Loss = ($300 - $295) - $1.50) x 100 = $350

The maximum profit, on the other hand, will be reached when the price of the underlying asset is equal to the strike price of the option sold or higher (on the right-hand side of the graph). The maximum loss is calculated as follows:

Maximum Profit = premium collected

In the example:

Maximum Profit = $150

When you sell a Bull Put the break-even point is calculated as follows:

Break-even Bull Put = Strike sold Put option - premium collected

In the example:

Break-even Bull Put = $300 - $1.50 = $298.50

Now I come to the two most important variables in options: time and volatility.

Time. You have seen that the time value part (extrinsic value) of the price of an option decreases as the expiration date approaches. This is a positive factor when you sell an option.

However, when you sell a Vertical Spread (both Bear Call and Bull Put), the sensitivity to time erosion depends on the relationship between the price of the underlying asset and the strike prices of the spread. If the price of the underlying asset is near ATM or OTM, relative to the option being sold, then the price of the Vertical Spread decreases with time. This happens because the option sold is closer to the price of the underlying and erodes faster than the option purchased further away.

If, on the other hand, the price of the underlying asset is near ATM or ITM relative to the option purchased, then the Vertical Spread increases as time passes. This happens because the Call option purchased is closer to the price of the underlying and erodes faster than the option sold. If the price of the underlying is halfway between the two strike prices, then time erosion has little effect on the price of the Vertical Spread because both the written and purchased options erode at approximately the same rate.

Volatility. When you sell an option, an increase in volatility leads to an increase in the price (premium) of the option and this is a negative factor. Conversely, a fall in volatility, even though the price of the underlying asset remains unchanged, leads to a loss in the value of the option sold.

When selling a Vertical Spread, if the price of the underlying is OTM relative to the option sold, a fall in volatility is a positive factor because the Vertical Spread decreases with volatility. This is because the option sold is closer to the price of the underlying and erodes faster than the option bought further away.

If, on the other hand, the price of the underlying asset is ATM or ITM relative to the option you have purchased, then an increase in volatility will be a positive factor as it will increase the value of the near-the-money option you have purchased faster than the in-the-money option you have sold, thereby decreasing the overall value of the spread.

To make the strategy more familiar, I will provide some examples, prefacing that I have not conducted any analysis of the underlying assets; these are merely examples intended to better explain how selling a Vertical Spread works.

Example #1

Convinced that Tesla will not make significant upward movements, I decide to take advantage of this by selling a Bear Call Spread, constructed by selling a Call option with a strike price of $210 and buying a Call option with a strike price of $215. Both options expire in 25 days; for selling the Call option, I collect a premium of $1.28, while for buying the Call option, I pay a premium of $0.95. In total, by selling the strategy, I collect a premium of $0.33. The broker requires a margin of $460 for a Return on Investment (ROI):

ROI = (Premium collected / Margin) x 100 = ($ 33 / $ 460) x 100 = 7.18%

In Figure 15, you can see Tesla's daily chart.

Figure 15 - Tesla daily chart (Mexem.com)

If at expiry the price of Tesla is equal to or less than $210, I will have secured the entire premium from the strategy.

Maximum profit = premium collected = $33

The maximum loss will occur if Tesla's price at option expiry is equal to or higher than the strike price of the purchased option (i.e., equal to or higher than $215). The maximum loss is calculated as follows:

Maximum loss = ((Bought Call strike – Sold Call strike) – premium collected) x 100

In the example with Tesla:

Maximum loss = (($215 – $210) – 0.33) x 100 = $467

The breakeven point is the Tesla price at which the operation neither gains nor loses money.

Bear Call breakeven point = Sold Call strike + premium collected

In the example with Tesla:

Bear Call breakeven point = $210 + $0.33 = $210.33

Example # 2

My outlook on the US stock market is bullish. So, after glancing at the SPY chart, the ETF of the S&P500 index, I decide to sell a Bull Put Spread, constructed by selling a Put option with a strike price of $490 and buying a Put option with a strike price of $485. Both options expire in 25 days. For selling the Put option, I collect a premium of $0.54, while for buying the Put option, I pay a premium of $0.42. In total, from selling the strategy, I collect a premium of $0.12. The margin required by the broker is $300 for an ROI:

ROI = (Premium collected / Margin) x 100 = ($ 12 / $ 300) x 100 = 4%

In Figure 16, you can see SPY's daily chart.

Figure 16 - SPY daily chart (Mexem.com)

I will collect the entire premium if at option expiry the price of SPY is $490 or higher.

Maximum profit = premium collected = $12

The maximum loss will occur if SPY's price at option expiry is equal to or lower than the strike price of the purchased option (i.e., equal to or higher than $485). The maximum loss is calculated as follows:

Maximum loss = ((Sold option strike - Bought option strike) - premium) x 100

In the example with SPY:

Maximum loss = ($490 - $485) - $0.12) x 100 = $488

The breakeven point, where the SPY strategy neither gains nor loses money, will be when the price is:

Bull Put breakeven point = Sold Call strike - premium collected

In the example with SPY:

Bull Put breakeven point = $490 - $0.12 = $489.88

Example #3

The last example concerns gold and more specifically the gold ETF GLD. You can see the chart in Figure 17.

Figure 17 - GLD daily chart (Mexem.com)

Favouring a continued retracement of gold from its highs in the coming weeks, I

43

decide to take advantage of this scenario by selling a Bear Call Spread, constructed by selling a Call option with a strike price of $225 and buying a Call option with a strike price of $230. Both options expire in 25 days; for selling the Call option, I collect a premium of $1.26, while for buying the Call option, I pay a premium of $0.57. In total, by selling the strategy, I collect a premium of $0.69. The broker requires a margin of $450 for an ROI:

ROI = (Premium collected / Margin) x 100 = ($ 69 / $ 450) x 100 = 15.33%

I will secure the entire premium if, at expiry, the price of GLD is equal to or less than $225.

Maximum profit = premium collected = $69

I will incur the maximum loss if GLD's price at option expiry is equal to or higher than the strike price of the purchased option (i.e., equal to or higher than $230). Specifically:

Maximum loss = ((Bought option strike - Sold option strike) - premium) x 100

In the example with GLD:

Maximum loss = ($230 - $225) - $0.69) x 100 = $431

The breakeven point is the GLD price at which the operation neither gains nor loses money.

Bear Call breakeven point = Sold Call strike + premium collected

In the example with GLD:

Bear Call breakeven point = $225 + $0.69 = $225.69

Some might frown upon these numbers, especially the strategy gains. Making $12 from the SPY strategy, what's the point? Unfortunately, the web is flooded with so-called gurus who tell you that you can get rich even with a few hundred euros. The truth is they are scamming you; if you want to make a certain profit, you need to have adequate capital, otherwise, it is no longer trading and becomes a lottery.

Investing $15,000 in the SPY strategy means selling 50 contracts and earning a premium of $600 in just 25 days, with very low risk. One such trade per month and by the end of the year, your $15,000 has become $22,200 (minus the still very low commissions). What other low-risk investment gives you a 48% profit in a year?

In conclusion, what you have just seen is the simplest and most common options strategy and, like all simple things, it is also the most widely used. It requires no special attention; the only somewhat more complicated aspect is correctly analysing the markets and finding opportunities to sell Vertical Spreads. This depends on you and your type of analysis.

BUYING A VERTICAL SPREAD

CHAPTER 8

You saw in the previous chapter that with a simple strategy, the Vertical Spread, you can sell options that, for a lower premium collected, it allows you to limit your losses.

Although selling options is certainly the best way to exploit this instrument, options can also be bought and so can the Vertical Spread. This allows you to pay a lower premium than the single naked option.

There are two strategies you can adopt depending on whether you are bullish or bearish on the underlying asset:

1. **Bull Call**. It consists of buying an ATM Call option and selling an OTM Call option with the same expiration date.

Let me show you an example of a Bull Call. I decide to buy an ATM Call option on IBM, strike $140, and sell an OTM Call option on IBM, strike $150. The expiration date is 21 January 2022. I pay a premium for the purchased option of $7.20 and collect a premium for the written option of $2.95. Therefore, the net premium I pay is $7.20 - $2.95 = $4.25 (i.e., $425).

When you buy a Bull Call, the performance is as follows (Figure 18):

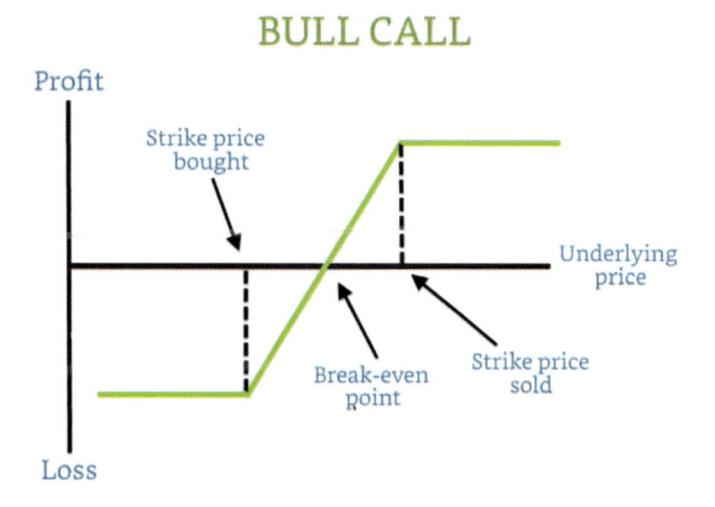

Figure 18 - Performance graph Bull Call

The maximum loss will occur when the price of the underlying asset is equal to the strike price of the option purchased or lower (on the left-hand side of the graph). The maximum loss is calculated as follows:

Maximum Loss = premium option bought - premium option sold

In the example with IBM:

Maximum Loss = $720 - $295 = $425

The maximum profit, on the other hand, will be achieved when the price of the underlying asset is equal to the strike price of the option sold or higher (on the right-hand side of the graph). The maximum loss is calculated as follows:

Maximum Profit = ((strike option sold - strike option bought) - premium) x 100

In the example:

Maximum Profit = (($150 - $140) - $4.25) x 100 = $575

Between the two strike prices, the lower the price of the underlying asset, the smaller the gain which, once past the break-even point, will turn into a loss.

When you sell a Bull Call the break-even point is calculated as follows:

Break-even Bull Call = Strike bought Call option + premium collected

In the example:

Break-even Bull Call = $140 + $4.25 = $144.25

2. Bear Put. It consists of buying an ATM Put option and selling another OTM Put option with the same expiration date.

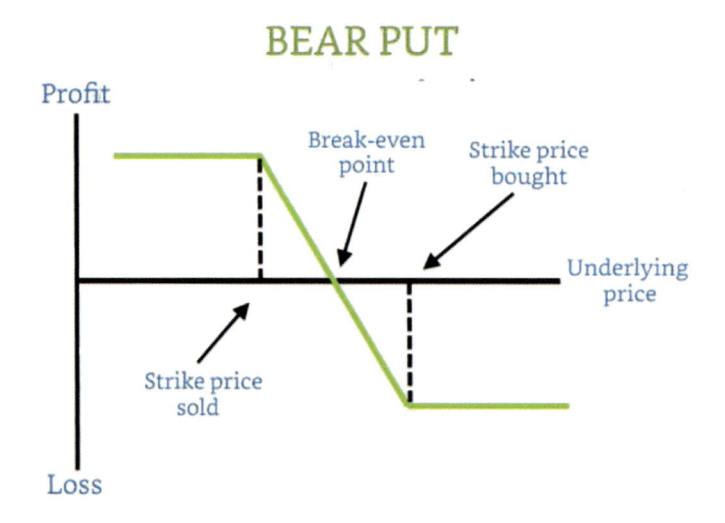

Figure 19 - Performance graph Bear Put

Let me show you an example of a Bear Put. I decide to buy an ATM Put option on Netflix, strike $640, and sell an OTM Put option on Netflix, strike $620. Expiration date 21 January 2022. I pay a premium for the purchased option of $47.40 and collect a premium for the written option of $37.10. Therefore, the net premium I pay is $47.40 - $37.10 = $10.30 ($1,030).

When you buy a Bear Put, the performance is as shown in Figure 19 above.

The maximum loss will occur when the price of the underlying asset is equal to the strike price of the option purchased or higher (on the right-hand side of the chart). The maximum loss is calculated as follows:

Maximum Loss = (premium option bought - premium option sold) x 100

In the example with Netflix:

Maximum Loss = ($47.40 - $37.10) = $1,030

The maximum profit, on the other hand, will be reached when the price of the underlying asset is equal to the strike price of the option sold or lower (on the left-hand side of the graph). The maximum loss is calculated as follows:

Maximum Profit = ((strike option bought - strike option sold) – premium) x 100

In the example:

Maximum Profit = (($640 - $620) - $10.30) x 100 = $970

Between the two strike prices, the higher the price of the underlying asset, the smaller the gain, which will turn into a loss once the break-even point has been crossed.

The breakeven point indicates the price of the underlying asset at which your trade neither gains nor loses money. When you buy a Bear Put the breakeven point is calculated as follows:

Break-even Bear Put = Strike bought Put option - premium paid

In the example:

Break-even point Bear Put = $640 - $10.30 = $629.70

As regards time and volatility, everything you saw with the sale of the Vertical Spread is reversed. In particular:

<u>Time</u>. You have already seen that the time value part (extrinsic value) of the price of an option decreases as the expiry date approaches. This is a negative factor when buying an option. However, equally, when you sell a Vertical Spread, as when you buy it (either Bull Call or Bear Put), the sensitivity to time erosion depends on the relationship between the price of the underlying asset and the strikes of the spread.

If the price of the underlying asset is near ATM or OTM, relative to the option bought, then the price of the Vertical Spread decreases over time. This happens because the option bought is closer to the price of the underlying asset and erodes faster than the option sold, which is further away.

If, on the other hand, the price of the underlying asset is close to ATM or ITM relative to the option written, then the Vertical Spread increases over time. This is because the Call option written is closer to the price of the underlying asset and erodes faster than the option bought. If the price of the underlying asset is halfway between the two strikes, then time erosion has little effect on the price of the Bull Call and Bear Put because both the written and bought options erode at roughly the same rate.

Volatility. When you buy an option, an increase in volatility leads to an increase in the price (premium) of the option and this is a positive factor. Conversely, a fall in volatility, even though the price of the underlying asset remains unchanged, leads to a loss in the value of the option purchased.

When selling a Vertical Spread, if the price of the underlying is OTM relative to the option bought, a fall in volatility is a negative factor because the Vertical Spread decreases with volatility. This is because the option bought is closer to the price of the underlying and erodes faster than the option sold further away.

If, on the other hand, the price of the underlying asset is near ATM or ITM relative to the option you have sold, then a decrease in volatility will be a positive factor as it will decrease the value of the near-the-money option you have sold faster than the in-the-money option you have bought, thereby increasing the overall value of the spread.

When you buy options, unlike when you sell them, you need low volatility to pay a lower premium. In addition, you need to identify where an underlying asset will move (and by a specific date). Of the two assumptions, the easier to identify is low volatility because to be certain of a good uptrend or downtrend, you need a crystal ball, which unfortunately no trader possesses.

Thus, buying an option with low implied volatility allows you to pay a lower premium, but it also means that at that moment, there is not much expectation on the underlying asset. On the contrary, with high implied volatility, the expectations for a movement of the underlying asset price are high, but the premium you will pay is also high. Implied volatility is a decisive factor in the choice of strategies.

At this point, you may be wondering: why buy a Vertical Spread and not just a Call or Put option? The strategy has pros and cons, and I will now show them to you with another example.

After my analysis I decided to buy SPY, the S&P 500 Index ETF. The current price is $439.19. I buy an ATM Call option, strike price $439 (closest to the current price), and sell an

OTM Call option, strike price $450. The expiration date is February 18, 2022. I pay a premium for the bought option of $18.35 and I collect a premium for the sold option of $12.00. Therefore, the net premium I pay is $18.35 - $12.00 = $6.35 ($635).

The first consideration is the maximum loss. Buying the Bull Call on SPY is $635. If I buy only the ATM Call option, my maximum risk (and loss) would be $1,835. So, by buying the Bull Call, I have a lower cost (<u>benefit</u>).

With the Bull Call, I have a break-even at $445.35 while with the purchase of the naked option, my break-even would be a little further away at $457.35 (<u>advantage</u>).

The profit from buying the Bull Call is the difference between the strike of the option sold ($450) minus the strike of the option purchased ($439) multiplied by 100 and minus the premium paid. In total, $475. With the purchase of the Call option, in theory, the profit, as you saw in Chapter 2, is unlimited (<u>disadvantage</u>).

However, if you think about it, when you open a trade, you also decide on a target for your operation; that is, where you will close the trade taking home the profits. No profitable trader buys a stock with the hope that it will rise for eternity (I am talking about trading, not investing, two very different things).

So, in summary, by buying a Vertical Spread, you are actually giving up a possible large profit that you could have by buying a Call option. However, you have the advantage of having a smaller maximum loss, you have a closer break-even point and the probability of profit is higher. It will be much more likely that at expiry the price will be in the $439/450 range rather than over $450.

However, always remember that there are no right and wrong strategies. It always depends on how and when they are used.

To complete the chapter, I will show you some examples to make this strategy very clear.

Example #1

Microsoft is about to surpass its all-time high, and I foresee this will give a strong bullish push. Therefore, I decide to take advantage of this scenario by buying a Bull Call Spread, constructed by buying a Call option with a strike price of $430 and selling a Call option with a strike price of $450. The expiration is in 25 days. For buying the Call, I pay a premium of $7.55, while for selling the Call, I collect a premium of $1.61, resulting in a total premium paid of $5.94, which represents the cost of the trade.

In Figure 20, you can see Microsoft's chart.

Figure 20 - Microsoft daily chart (Mexem.com)

The maximum loss will occur when Microsoft's price is equal to or lower than the strike price of the purchased option (i.e., $430). The maximum loss is calculated as follows:

Maximum loss = (premium of bought option - premium of sold option) x 100

In the example with Microsoft:

Maximum loss = ($7.55 - $1.61) x 100 = $594

The maximum profit, on the other hand, will be achieved when Microsoft's price is equal to or higher than the strike price of the sold option (i.e., $450). The maximum profit is calculated as follows:

Maximum profit = ((strike of sold option - strike of bought option) – premium) x 100

In the example with Microsoft:

Maximum profit = (($450 - $430) - $5.94) x 100 = $1,406

When you buy a Bull Call Spread, the breakeven point is calculated as follows:

Bull Call Breakeven = Strike of bought Call option + premium paid

In the example with Microsoft:

Bull Call Breakeven = $430 + $5.94 = $430.94

Therefore, my trade will start to make a profit once Microsoft's price exceeds $430.94.

Example #2

A stock that my analysis suggests is strongly bearish is Verizon, and I take advantage of this by buying a Bear Put Spread, constructed by buying a Put option with a strike price of $39 and selling a Put option with a strike price of $37. To buy the Put option, I pay a premium of $0.48, while for selling the Put option, I collect $0.11, for a total cost of the strategy of $0.37.

In Figure 21, you can see Verizon's chart.

Figure 21 - Verizon daily chart (Mexem.com)

The maximum loss will occur when Verizon's price is equal to or higher than the strike price of the purchased option. The maximum loss is calculated as follows:

Maximum loss = (premium of bought option - premium of sold option) x 100

In the example with Verizon:

Maximum loss = ($0.48 - $0.11) x 100 = $37

The maximum profit, on the other hand, will be achieved when Verizon's price is equal to or lower than the strike price of the sold option. The maximum profit is calculated as follows:

Maximum profit = ((strike of bought option - strike of sold option) – premium) x 100

In the example with Verizon:

Maximum profit = (($39 - $37) - $0.37) x 100 = $163

Between the two strike prices, the higher Verizon's price, the lower the profit, which, once past the breakeven point, will turn into a loss.

The breakeven point indicates the price of the underlying asset at which your trade neither gains nor loses money. When buying a Bear Put Spread, the breakeven point is calculated as follows:

Bear Put Breakeven = Strike of bought Put option - premium paid

In the example with Verizon:

Bear Put Breakeven = $39 - $0.37 = $38.63

My trade will start to make a profit once Verizon's price drops below $38.63.

Example #3

I am convinced that crude oil will soon start a strong rally that will bring it at least to the $85 area. Therefore, I take advantage of this (potential) rise in the futures contract by buying a Bull Call Spread, constructed by buying a Call option with a strike price of $80 and selling a Call option with a strike price of $85. The premium paid for buying the Call option is $2.45, and the premium collected for selling the Call option is $0.83, resulting in a total premium paid (and cost of the trade) of $1.62.

Important: The premium I pay or collect with an option on the crude oil futures contract is per barrel. The crude oil futures contract size is 1,000 barrels, so the cost of the trade ($1.62) must be multiplied by 1,000 instead of 100.

In Figure 22, you can see the crude oil chart.

Figure 22 - Crude oil daily chart (Mexem.com)

The maximum loss will occur when the price of crude oil is equal to or lower than the strike price of the purchased option (i.e., $80).

Maximum loss = (premium of bought option - premium of sold option) x 1,000

In the example with Crude oil:

Maximum loss = ($2.45 - $0.83) x 1,000 = $1,620

The maximum profit, on the other hand, will be achieved when the price of crude oil is equal to or higher than the strike price of the sold option (i.e., $85). The maximum profit is calculated as follows:

Maximum profit = ((strike of sold option - strike of bought option) – premium) x 1,000

In the example with Crude oil:

Maximum profit = (($85 - $80) - $1.62) x 1,000 = $3,380

When you buy a Bull Call Spread, the breakeven point is calculated as follows:

Bull Call Breakeven = Strike of bought Call option + premium paid

In the example with Crude oil:

Bull Call Breakeven = $80 + $1.62 = $81.62

Quindi, inizierò a veder guadagnare la mia operazione una volta che il prezzo del crude oil avrà superato $81.62.

At the end of this chapter, I will give you a new definition (yes, I know, there are a lot of definitions regarding options). When you buy a Vertical Spread, that spread is a "Debit Spread" because you are buying an option with a higher premium and simultaneously selling an option with a lower premium (so you have to pay a premium to open your strategy).

Conversely, when you sell a Vertical Spread, that spread is a "Credit Spread" because you are selling an option with a higher premium and simultaneously buying an option with a lower premium (so, from that strategy, you will collect a premium).

Now that you have seen how to build a Vertical Spread, both buying and selling, the next step is to figure out which options (strike prices) to use.

Choose the Right Options

CHAPTER 9

~

You have seen the simplest of all options strategies, the Vertical Spread. However, there are still two things you need to decide in order to complete your trade: choosing the right strikes and how to handle any losses (stop-loss). You will see in this chapter how to choose the correct strikes to build a Vertical Spread. In the next chapter, you will see two stop-loss strategies.

When you buy a Vertical Spread the choice is simple, you buy the ATM option and sell the strike which represents your target. It is not so simple when you sell a Vertical Spread. For example, if you want to sell short Goldman Sachs stock (current price $393.60) with a target of $370, you have to build the Bear Put by buying the ATM Put option, strike $395 (the strike closest to the current price), and selling the OTM Put option, strike $370. Very simple.

Figure 23 - Boeing Company daily chart support (TradingView)

Let me premise, for those who do not know me, that I do not use technical analysis, so do not expect Bollinger Bands, RSI, divergences, and other indicators or patterns. However, there is one aspect of technical analysis you can use, initially. I am talking about support and resistance levels. Let's look at supports and resistances, starting with the definition.

A level is defined as "**support**" when demand is particularly strong and sellers are unable to overcome it. A support level is all the more significant if it has been tested several times in the past without being broken. Thus, support reflects the inability of a market to fall below a certain price level. You can see an example of support in the chart of the Boeing Company (Figure 23 above).

A level is called "**resistance**" when the supply is particularly strong, and buyers cannot win against sellers. A resistance level becomes more significant the more times it has been tested in the past without being broken. Thus, resistance reflects the inability of a market to rise above a certain price level. You can see an example of resistance in the Walmart chart (Figure 24).

Figure 24 - Walmart daily chart resistance (TradingView)

If you know me, you will know very well that I do not use technical analysis, including supports and resistances. However, since everyone is free to trade as they see fit, I will give a brief description of supports and resistances below.

There are two types of support/resistance: static and dynamic.

- A "**static**" support/resistance level corresponds to a precise and constant point in time (as you have seen in the two charts above), such as the high and low of the year, or a Fibonacci retracement.

- A "**dynamic**" support/resistance level, instead, changes its value as time passes.

Below, you can see an example of dynamic support with the daily chart of eBay (Figure 25).

Figure 25 - eBay daily chart dynamic support (TradingView)

Supports and resistances over time tend to be overcome, in such cases, an old resistance becomes new support, and past support turns into new resistance. There is a *change of polarity*, as shown in the Skyworks Solutions chart (Figure 26).

Figure 26 - Skyworks Solutions change of polarity (TradingView)

From the Skyworks Solutions chart above, you can see how $174, at the beginning of the chart, was a resistance for a price, then a support, and at the end of the chart again a resistance.

The only supports and resistances that you have to consider are the static ones that you can use to find levels that an underlying asset has difficulty overcoming.

What you need to do is sell a Call option or a Put option at a strike price that you think the underlying asset will not reach before the expiration date. I show you an example. In Figure 27 you can see the Vertex Pharmaceutical Incorporated daily chart.

Figure 27 - Vertex Pharmaceutical Incorporated daily chart *(TradingView)*

If I decide to sell a Bear Call, at what strike should I sell the Call option? Well, I certainly will not sell a strike below resistance, where the price of the underlying asset can come in unimpeded, but rather above, where it is more difficult for the option to go in-the-money, for example, $210.

As a rule, never sell a Call option immediately below resistance and never sell a Put option immediately above support. You must always sell an option where you think the strike cannot be reached by the price of the underlying asset.

When you choose the options with which to build the Vertical Spread to sell, you need to look at another Greek, the Delta.

Delta (δ) is one of the most commonly used Greeks in options trading. You have already seen another Greek, Theta, in Chapter 2 which tells you how much time your option has left. Delta, on the other hand, tells you how much chance the market gives the underlying asset of reaching the strike on the expiration date.

My advice is to always sell options with a Delta of less than 20. It means that the market gives less than a 20% chance for the underlying asset to reach the strike on the expiration date.

Another aspect you need to consider is open interest. Open interest represents the total number of open futures contracts on an underlying asset. My advice is to select strikes with an open interest of at least a thousand contracts; that way, if you need to close the trade, you will not have any difficulty doing so.

At this point, having looked at what you need to consider when choosing the strike of the option you have sold, let's see what strike you need to choose for the option you want to buy so that you can build your Vertical Spread.

The choice is very simple and purely economic. If you hedge the written option with a strike far away, you will have a more significant premium against a larger margin (and a larger maximum loss). The reason is that hedging with a distant strike means exposing yourself to greater risk.

As is often the case, practice is better than theory. So let me show you a couple of examples.

First example. I decide to sell a Bear Call on Vertex Pharmaceutical built by selling the Call option strike for $210 and buying the Call option strike for $220. The expiration date is December 17, 2021.

From this strategy, I collect a premium of $0.80 (i.e., $80). Doing the calculations, you can see that my maximum risk (which also coincides with the margin required by the broker) is:

Max Loss = ($220 - $210) x 100 - $80 = $920

So, we have an ROI (Return on Investment) of 8.70%, that is:

($80 / $920) x 100 = 8.70%

Second example. I build the Bear Call on Vertex Pharmaceutical by always selling the Call option strike $210, but, this time, I decide to buy the Call option with strike $230. I collect a higher premium, $130. Doing the same calculation:

Max Loss = ($230 – $210) x 100 - $130 = $1,870

So, we have an ROI of 6,95%, that is:

($130/$1,870 x 100) = 6,95%

You have seen with the two previous examples that if you have to choose one of the two operations, it is without a doubt more advantageous the first one: you face a smaller risk and you obtain a better ROI.

Therefore, for a matter of convenience, for purely economic reasons, at least in the first phase of learning, it is always better, when you create a Vertical Spread, to hedge the written option with the first available strike price.

To summarise, when you buy a Vertical Spread, whether Bull Call or Bear Put, you must buy the at-the-money (ATM) strike and sell the out-the-money (OTM) strike which represents your take profit.

When you sell a Vertical Spread, whether Bull Put or Bear Call, you need to make some considerations and evaluations about the option you are selling. As for the option to buy, you simply choose the first available strike price. A choice that as you have seen is purely economic.

At this point, to complete the first part, there are only a few considerations about entering the market and stop-loss, which you will see in the next chapter.

Stop-Loss Strategies

CHAPTER 10

Before talking about stop-loss, I want to briefly touch on the entry price and how to exploit daily fluctuations in option prices.

Options move much more during the course of a day than the underlying asset. It is all but rare to see an option move 15-20% with a 1/1.5% change in the price of the underlying asset. This is due to volatility and acceleration which amplify the movement. You will see more about acceleration in Chapter 20.

So, what strategy should you adopt? A lot depends on how many contracts you intend to open: one or more than one; a decision that has to be made according to your money management.

If you only plan to open one contract, my advice is to place an entry price 15-20% away from the current price. So, for example, if you have decided to sell a Bear Call and it has a current price of $0.60, then you should place the entry price at $0.70, thereby trying to take advantage of the daily volatility of the options.

You will certainly open fewer trades in this way, but you will also be more profitable with a higher percentage of profit. I can assure you, from experience, that only this little trick will allow you to make a profit of several hundred dollars more every year.

Always remember that it is not true that "more trades" translates into "more profit." In fact, quite often, the opposite is true. That is why I advise you to take advantage of the price fluctuations that the options market offers you. In addition, a better entry price allows you to manage your trade better if the underlying asset moves against you.

If, on the other hand, you can open more than one contract, then it is better to diversify your market entries. If you decide to sell the Bear Call in the example above with four contracts, you can sell one at the current price. In this way, you are in the trade if the underlying asset starts a bearish trend.

Then, you can sell a second contract at $0.70 and the others always at a distance of 10/15% from the previous entry price, so, $0.80 and $0.90. This way, as mentioned, you have a better handle on the trade, with a better average entry price. Of course, you can decide otherwise, depending on your trading style and experience.

Now, it is time to talk about stop-loss. You have seen that when you sell a Vertical Spread your maximum loss is no longer unlimited. However, you can further reduce your risk (and loss) by placing a stop-loss.

In this chapter, you will see a couple of strategies. However, let me first say that there is no one stop-loss suitable for all options strategies, but you must apply the stop-loss that best suits the strategy you are using.

First stop-loss strategy. It consists in selling a Vertical Spread with the stop-loss placed on the whole strategy. It is very simple, and I will show you an example.

You decide to sell a Bull Put on Netflix and collect a premium of $200. What you need to do is to place a stop-loss at three times the premium collected, i.e., $600. In this way, your maximum loss is:

$600 (stop-loss) - $200 (premium collected) = $400 (max loss)

So, once you have sold the Bull Put, you need to place a stop-loss at three times the premium collected. This way, your maximum loss will be twice the premium. Unlike other assets such as stocks, currencies, commodities, etc., when you sell options, you do not have an R/R (Risk/Risk) in your favour. But even working under these conditions, you can make a profit, month after month, year after year.

I will demonstrate this with an example. You sell three Vertical Spreads and for each of these strategies you collect a $100 premium. Two of them close worthless and one closes at the stop-loss price. So, you have a profit of $200 with the first two strategies and a loss of $200 with the third, a percentage of 66% (2 out of 3).

At first glance, this may seem an unsatisfactory result. "66% of my options strategies have to close worthless just to break even". If you are thinking this, you are forgetting another important thing. Your odds of profit are higher than 66%.

The initial probability of selling options is 75%. But you are not reading this book for initial probability, otherwise, you would not need to do this, nor would you need to learn. You are here to aim higher than just 75%. Your goal is to get at least 85%.

At this point some of you are thinking well, instead of placing the stop-loss three times the premium, I will put it twice the premium, so I will have lower losses. Actually, this is not true. As mentioned at the beginning of the chapter, during the day, options have significant price fluctuations, and placing a stop-loss too close to the current price would cause you to close too many trades at a loss.

Putting a stop-loss on the whole Vertical Spread is a conservative strategy because it protects the trade and allows you to close the Vertical Spread with both options, leaving nothing open. In this way, you have a certain and predictable loss; you already know how much you will lose.

Second stop-loss strategy. This strategy consists of selling a Vertical Spread with the stop-loss placed on the sold option only. This is a more aggressive strategy that allows you to manage the option you have bought if the underlying asset continues its trend. However, with this type of stop-loss, you do not have a certain and predictable loss because you do not know how much you will gain from the option you bought (and more importantly, if you will gain).

I will show you more concretely how to earn from the option you bought with an example. You always sell a Bull Put on Netflix; you collect a premium of $1,240 for the option you sold and pay $1,020 for the one you bought. So, you collect a total premium of $220. The maximum loss with the stop-loss on the Vertical Spread, as you have already seen, is $440 (twice the premium collected).

By placing the stop-loss on the written option only, you would place it at three times the premium collected, i.e., $3,720. After one month, the written option closes at the stop-loss price, so you have a loss of $2,480 ($3,720 minus $1,240 in premium collected). Conversely, the option you bought at $1,020 is now worth $3,060, giving you a gain of $2,040. So, you are in the situation you budgeted for with the stop-loss on the whole Vertical Spread, a total loss of $440 ($2,480 loss on the written option minus a $2,040 gain on the one you bought).

But you still have the option you bought in your portfolio and with it, you could also make a profit of $3,000, $4,000, or more, completely reversing your loss on the written option. Similarly, it could also fall to $1,500, $1,000, or less, and in that case, it would give you a total loss well in excess of $440, which was the expected amount. You do not know what the underlying asset will do in the next few weeks. So how should you proceed?

You need to look at the chart. If the stop-loss on the written option was reached through a major breakout of support or resistance, my advice is to hold the purchased option for at least a week because if the underlying asset starts a trend, you have a "lottery ticket" in your hand.

If after a week the underlying asset is not moving in a trend, then it is advisable to close the option you bought as well, so that your loss does not increase. As for the latter, there is another situation which can give you a "lottery ticket". Look at the next example.

You decide to sell a Bull Put on Walt Disney. You collect a premium of $140 for the written option and pay a premium of $80 for the purchased one. So, you collect a total premium of $60.

After one month, the written option lost $95, and the purchased option lost $70.

The expiration date is still three weeks away. At this point, you may decide to close the written option and collect the $45 premium and leave the purchased option in the portfolio, which has lost $70 and is now only worth $10.

In this way, you have collected a secure premium of $45 instead of $60, but you have closed the trade three weeks before expiration (with the possibility of diverting the used margin to another trade), and you still have the purchased option in your portfolio that will most likely expire worthless but could also give you great satisfaction.

In fact, all it takes is one winning ticket to pay you 20, 50, or 100 times that $5 or $10 profit you lost because you kept the purchased option in your portfolio. In a theoretical course, it is not an easy subject to deal with but I assure you that statistically, it is something that happens. Personally, I win on average a couple of "lotteries" a year.

It becomes more complicated to decide on a stop-loss when you **buy a Vertical Spread**. But first, let me clarify an aspect.

When you buy a Vertical Spread, unlike when you sell it, you are directional and it is not easy to give precise rules. It can also happen that you place a stop-loss, the Vertical Spread reaches that price the day after (it has happened to me in past), and then, the underlying asset makes a great explosion in your direction, and you curse against the market, the broker, the platform... Hehe.

Personally, when I buy a Vertical Spread, I prefer not to put the stop-loss on the platform, but manage it manually. In the sense that, if I see that the trade will probably not bear fruit, then I close it. So, if the trade has lost 70%, 80%, or 90% of the premium paid, I close the position to take home the few dollars of premium, so as not to leave it in the market.

However, if you want to try to give a rule that gives you a direction to follow, at least initially for your tests in the demo platform, you can use a strategy similar to the one you saw in selling a Vertical Spread.

Let me show you an example. You buy a Bull Call on Apple and pay a premium of $150. You can put a stop-loss on the Vertical Spread if it loses at least two-thirds of its value. So, if the $150 premium falls to $50, you close the trade. This is because it is statistically difficult for the Bull Call to recover its loss and give you a profit.

Before concluding this chapter, I would like to say a few words about the expiration date. Options are like a vegetable garden where you have to let the plants grow to bear fruit. In the same way, you need to give your strategies time to mature. But how long?

There is no precise rule, it depends on the time perspective of your trade. It is a bit easier to decide on an expiration date when selling a Vertical Spread. In this case, my advice is to choose an expiration date of at least 45 days, for several reasons. You collect a higher premium from a higher time value. If the underlying asset initially moves against you, the movement is unlikely to be so strong as to reach the stop-loss price. You have time to adjust your strategy.

The situation is different when you buy a Vertical Spread because you are directional and need to be able to identify the moment when the underlying asset rises or falls. The choice is yours based on your analysis. I will conclude by reminding you that you are not obliged to hold options in your portfolio until the expiration date.

In the following chapters, you will see other options strategies, the most commonly used ones.

MANAGE OF A CREDIT SPREAD

CHAPTER 11

~

I would like to promise you that if you learn what I have written in this book well, every single strategy you use will give you a profit, but I would be a liar. However, I can say that with most of them you will make a profit. But what really makes the difference between a trader who spends all day in front of a monitor and a trader who works like a pro are the strategies that do not go in the right direction.

After all, the same is true in every area of life; in fact, a person is not judged when everything is going well, but when things start to go wrong because it is during adversity that one shows what one is made of.

I would like to stress that you cannot theorise what to do when the market goes against you because it depends on the specific situation. Markets change all the time and it would be presumptuous of me to think that a book can give you the one-size-fits-all solution. However, you have to try to understand what you might do if a strategy goes against you; for example, if a Bear Call sold doubles the premium you collected.

So, through an example, I will show you the different ways in which you can manage a losing strategy.

Imagine you have decided to sell a Bull Put on Facebook (now Meta Platforms Inc.), constructed by selling a Put option with a strike price of $170 and buying a Put option with a strike price of $165. The expiry date is 21 April 2023 and the premium collected is $110. In the following days, the price of Facebook declines, and your Bull Put now has a premium of $220, which is double what you had collected from the sale of the strategy.

Strategy #1

Here is the situation:

- Premium collected from selling the Bull Put: $110;
- Current premium of the strategy: $220;
- Current loss: $110 (Current Premium $220 - Initial Premium $110).

If your analysis has not changed and the conditions remain the same, the first decision you can make is to roll over the strategy with the same strike prices to the next expiration date.

What does "rolling over the strategy" mean?

1. **Close the current trade**: close the current Bull Put realising a loss of $110. This means you buy the Bull Put spread at the current price of $220.
2. **Open a new Bull Put**: reopen the same strategy, with the same strike prices ($170 and $165), but with a new expiration date of 19 May 2023. This time, you collect a premium of $150.

This is the new situation:

- New premium collected: $150;
- Previous loss: $110;
- Total balance: $150 (new premium) - $110 (previous loss) = $40 net profit.

Now let's look at the advantages and disadvantages of this strategy.

- ✓ **PRO**. By rolling over the strategy, you have the opportunity to turn a loss into a profit. The loss incurred from the previous strategy ($110) is more than covered by the premium collected from selling the new Bull Put ($150), resulting in a net profit of $40.
- ✓ **CON**. However, you extend the risk of further losses. If the price of Facebook continues to decline, your new strategy could become a losing one again, and you will face the dilemma of whether to continue rolling over the strategy or close the trade with a greater loss.

The decision to roll over a trade can be an effective strategy to recover a losing position, but it must be supported by solid analysis indicating an imminent trend reversal. Otherwise, you risk falling into the trap of hope, which is never a good trading strategy.

Strategy #2

An alternative to this method, which I consider quite aggressive, is to roll the strategy but using different strike prices. The situation is similar to the previous one, but instead of just rolling the strategy to the next expiration month, you also adjust the strikes. I will show you how to do this using the same Facebook example as above.

Here is the situation:

- Premium collected from the Bull Put sale: $110;
- Current strategy premium: $220;
- Current loss: $110 (Current Premium $220 - Initial Premium $110).

You might decide to use a variant of the previous method as follows:

1. **Close the Current Trade**: close the current Bull Put, realising a loss of $110. This means buying the Bull Put spread at the current price of $220.
2. **Open a New Bull Put**: reopen the same strategy with different strike prices (sell the $160 Put and buy the $155 Put) and a new expiration date of 19th May 2023. This time, you collect a premium of $115.

This time, not only have you rolled the strategy to the next expiration date, from March '23 to May '23, but you have also adjusted the strikes from $170/$165 to $160/$155. There is no absolute rule on which strikes to choose; the important thing is that the premium collected from the new strategy roughly matches the loss from the old strategy (preferably including commissions).

Let's look at the advantages and disadvantages of this strategy.

✓ **PRO**: this strategy allows you to recover your losses with a higher probability (and less risk) compared to the previous method, as you also adjust the strike prices further away from the current price of the underlying asset.
✓ **CON**: with this method, your maximum profit is what you lost with the previous strategy, thus forgoing the opportunity to turn the trade to your advantage.

The decision to roll a trade by moving not only the expiration date but also the strike prices can be an effective and less risky strategy to recover a losing position. However, this choice implies forgoing a potential gain upfront and focusing solely on recovering the loss. It must be supported by a solid analysis showing that the initial conditions have not changed and indicating a likely trend reversal.

Strategy #3

Another even more conservative method is to create a Short Iron Condor when the premium becomes double that initially collected. The Short Iron Condor is another options strategy that you will see in the next chapter. I will explain this method using the same Facebook example as before.

Here is the situation:

- Premium collected from the Bull Put sale: $110;
- Current strategy premium: $220;
- Current loss: $110 (Current Premium $220 - Initial Premium $110).

This time, instead of closing the strategy and opening a new one, you sell another Vertical Spread.

1. **Keep the Bull Put open**: maintain the Bull Put with the same strikes and expiration date.
2. **Sell a Bear Call**: sell a Call option with a strike of $200 and buy a Call option with a strike of $205 (the expiration date is 21 April '23). From this strategy, you collect a premium of $65.

You decide to keep the Bull Put open and sell a Bear Call, thus completing a Short Iron Condor, constructed by selling a Bull Put and a Bear Call either simultaneously or sequentially. By doing so, your current loss decreases to $45 (Current Premium $220 - Initial Premium $110 - Bear Call Premium $65).

Now let's look at the advantages and disadvantages of this strategy.

- ✓ **PRO**: with this method, you at least limit the loss of the original strategy without using additional capital, as opening two opposite positions will not increase the margin required by the broker. If Facebook rebounds and starts to rise, you can double your profit by collecting the premium from both the Bull Put and the Bear Call.
- ✓ **CON**: however, with this method, it is not guaranteed that you will recover the entire loss of the original strategy. It is possible that you will achieve only a reduction of the losses from the Bull Put sale (an aspect not to be underestimated).

This strategy is more suited to a rather slow-moving underlying asset, allowing you to structure the Short Iron Condor intelligently with the aim of collecting the highest possible premium. You need to be adept at managing the entire trade, which has changed from what you had originally planned.

Strategy #4

A fourth and final strategy I will outline for reversing a wrong trade is to close the sold option and keep the bought option open. This method should only be used if the initial conditions have changed. I will show you how to do this using the same Facebook example as in the previous strategies.

Here is the situation:

- Premium collected from the Bull Put sale: $110;
- Current strategy premium: $220;
- Current loss: $110 (Current Premium $220 - Initial Premium $110).

With this strategy, you do not close the Bull Put to reopen it with different strike prices and expiration dates, but rather you only close the sold Put option.

1. **Close the sold option**: Buy the Put option with a $170 strike price at market to close your short position.
2. **Keep the bought option open**: Keep the Put option with a $165 strike price open.

You decide to close the sold Put option with a $170 strike price, realising a loss, but deliberately keep the bought Put option with a $165 strike price open.

Let's look at the advantages and disadvantages of this strategy.

- ✓ **PRO**: if Facebook's price continues to fall, the bought Put option can significantly increase in value, allowing you to recover the loss or even make a profit.

- ✓ **CON**: if the underlying asset's price rebounds instead of continuing to fall, you could incur further losses as the bought Put option will decrease in value.

This strategy is more suited to experienced traders who can closely monitor the market and have a clear understanding of the dynamics at play. It requires precise timing and solid market analysis to be effective. It should be used cautiously and only when there are strong indications that market conditions are changing significantly.

In conclusion, the strategies outlined above are just a few of the simpler methods for managing a losing strategy with a Credit Spread. There are others which I will not explain as they require more experience. After all, this book is a guide for beginners.

You cannot decide in advance which method to use because it is impossible to predict an event before it happens; each situation is different and must be managed accordingly. You need to assess the trade, understand if your analysis is still valid or if something has changed. Understand why you are losing and implement the best strategy to at least limit the loss.

It is crucial to know how to manage a losing trade because even limiting a loss is a success, for you and for your trading. Believe me, this will make a significant difference at the end of the year.

PART THREE: SOME STRATEGIES

Short Iron Condor

CHAPTER 12

At the end of the previous chapter, I mentioned a new strategy, the Short Iron Condor. The Short Iron Condor is a strategy built by selling two Vertical Spreads, a Bull Put and a Short Call. You use the Short Iron Condor when you expect the price of the underlying asset to move within a narrow range during the options' lifespan.

Strategy: it is a four-part strategy consisting of a bull Put spread, and a bear Call spread in which the Call strikes are above, and the Put strikes below the current level of the underlying asset price. The distance between the Call strikes equals the distance between the Put strikes and all options have the same expiration date. The strategy that you have always to sell on the platform.

Max Gain: Short Iron Condor is a credit strategy, so, your maximum profit is the premium collected for buying the strategy. It is realised if the underlying is equal to or between the strike price of the short options on the expiration date, in which case all options expire worthless, and the premium is kept as income.

Max Gain = premium collected

Max Loss: the maximum risk is equal to the difference between the two strikes of the Bull Put (or Bear Call) less the premium collected. There are two possible outcomes in which the maximum loss is realised. **1.** If the underlying is below the lower strike at expiration, then the Call options expire worthless, but both Put ones are in the money (and so, the Bull Put reaches its maximum value). **2.** If the underlying is above the highest strike at expiration, then the Put options expire worthless, but both Call options are in the money (and in this case, the Bear Call reaches its maximum value).

Max Loss = (Put highest strike - Put lowest strike) x 100 - premium collected

or

Max Loss = (Call highest strike - Call lowest strike) x 100 - premium collected

Break-even: there are two break-even points. The lower break-even point is the underlying asset price equal to the strike price of the short Put option minus the premium collected. The upper break-even point is the underlying asset price same to the strike price of the short Call option plus the premium collected.

Lower break-even = short Put strike - premium collected

Upper break-even = short Call strike + premium collected

<u>Time Decay</u>: when you sell a Long Iron Condor, you are selling two Vertical Spreads, a Bear Call and a Bull Put, and you have seen that Short Vertical Spread has a Theta positive so the passage of time will help this strategy.

<u>Volatility</u>: you have seen that Short Vertical Spread has a Vega negative, so the Short Iron Condor spread loses money when volatility rises. When volatility falls, the Short Iron Condor spread makes money. I will explain the Vega in a few pages.

<u>Stop-loss</u>: on the strategy when the premium collected tripled its value.

When you sell a Short Iron Condor, the performance is as follows (Figure 28):

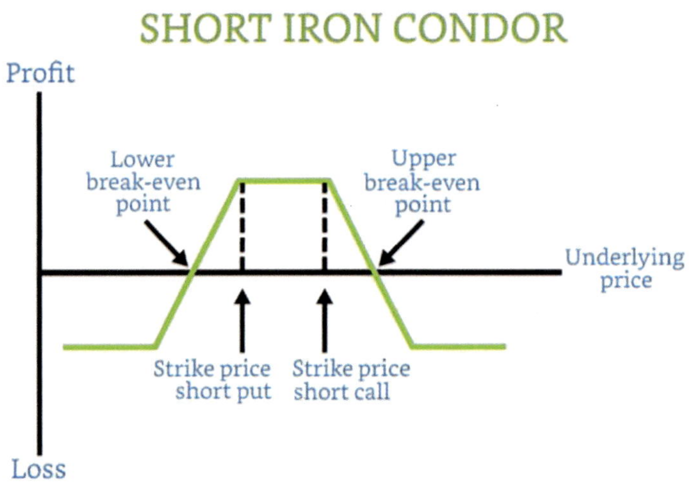

Figure 28 - Performance graph Short Iron Condor

Now I show you an example to understand better this strategy.

In Figure 29, you can see the chart of Meta (price $470.81), which I predict will move sideways within a range between $405 (support) and $525 (resistance) in the coming weeks. Therefore, I decide to take advantage of this sideways movement by selling a Short Iron Condor.

I sell a Bull Put constructed by selling the Put option, strike $405, expiring in 33 days, and buying the Put option, strike $400, also expiring in 33 days. At the same time, I sell a Short Call constructed by selling the Call option, strike $525, also expiring in 33 days, and buying the Call option, strike $530, expiring in 33 days.

Figure 29 - Meta daily chart (Mexem.com)

With the sale of the Bull Put, I collect a premium of $0.32, while with the sale of the Bear Call, I collect a premium of $0.50. So, in total, I collect a premium from the strategy of $0.82 per share ($82 in total). The margin required by the broker for the Short Iron Condor is $370, resulting in an ROI of:

ROI = ($82 / $370) x 100 = 22.16%

The maximum loss occurs when the price of the underlying asset rises above the strike of the purchased Call option, i.e., $530, or falls below the strike of the purchased Put option, i.e., $400.

In the example with Meta:

Maximum Loss = (($405 – $400) x 100) – $82 (premium collected) = $418

or

Maximum Loss = (($530 – $525) x 100) – $82 (premium collected) = $418

The maximum profit, being a credit strategy, is given by the premiums collected and occurs when the price of the underlying asset is between the two strike prices of the options sold.

In the example with Meta:

Maximum Profit = $32 (Bull Put premium) + $50 (Bear Call premium) = $82

There are two break-even points. The lower break-even occurs when the price of the underlying asset equals the strike of the Put option sold minus the collected premium. The upper break-even occurs when the price of the underlying asset equals the strike of the Call option sold plus the collected premium.

In the example with Meta:

Lower Break-even = $405 – $0,32 (Bull Put premium) = $404,68

Upper Break-even = $525 + $0,50 (Short Call premium) = $525,50

Although the Short Iron Condor is a profitable strategy, it is essential to understand how it works as it can incur losses if used incorrectly. The advantages of the Short Iron Condor are numerous, with its non-directionality being the foremost. This is perhaps its greatest advantage, distinguishing it from other options trading strategies. You do not need to predict the market's direction or determine the exact distance the security will move. Instead, you are establishing a price range within which the trade will succeed.

This range is the distance between the strikes of the two options, Call and Put, that are sold. The wider the range between the two sold options, the higher the probability of profit, but simultaneously, the lower your profit potential. However, since it is a high-success-rate operation, the lower profit (still an acceptable percentage) is not a significant disadvantage. The only thing to always keep an eye on is the potential lack of liquidity when establishing a very wide range.

Resist the temptation to chase high returns, exceeding 5%. Instead, aim for a range between 3% and 5%, as this will ensure you consistent income over time in a repeatable and scalable manner. It is not necessary to implement Short Iron Condors on the stocks you own; in fact, I advise against it. For that purpose, as you will see in Chapter 14, another strategy, the Covered Call, is much more suitable.

The Short Iron Condor [works in all market conditions](), meaning it is an excellent strategy to use regardless of the underlying asset's performance. Whether it is a bullish, bearish, or broadly sideways market, the strategy will always work and generate a profit. While it is ideal to employ this strategy when the underlying asset is moving sideways, remember that trending markets can also exhibit significant sideways movements within them.

This strategy is the combination of two net credit spread operations, giving you the opportunity to earn two premiums, from a Bear Call and a Bull Put. Since both sides of the trade cancel out each other's directional bias, it is a great deal. Essentially, you are paid to maintain a neutral spread on the markets with lower risk, and therefore with a more limited maximum loss, compared to a simple vertical spread.

The lack of directional bias also means the strategy has [lower maintenance requirements](). Although there are adjustments you can make in the Short Iron Condor, if the sold strikes have been chosen correctly, you will find that you will not need to monitor the trade more than once a day, without needing to adjust it. You can even opt not to directly manage the trade by setting price alerts within the trading platform when the underlying approaches the sold strikes. This way, you have the opportunity to assess whether it is necessary to adjust the spread or not without having to spend the whole day in front of the screen. Therefore, the Short Iron Condor is a suitable strategy for those who trade part-time, alongside another job.

Short Iron Condors typically do not need much adjustment. Even if an adjustment is necessary, it often involves widening the spread of one of the two credit spreads. In the short term, you may incur a loss, but subsequent operations tend to recover the adjustment cost. You will have a better understanding of how to adjust a Short Iron Condor in the next chapter.

Now let's look at how to structure the Short Iron Condor. There are two ways, the first, and the best if you are a novice, is to ensure that the price of the underlying asset is at the centre of the range of sold strikes (or as close to it as possible). This way, the two strikes will be equidistant from each other, ensuring complete neutrality.

If you are a more experienced trader and comfortable with this strategy, you can choose to sell the two credit spreads at different times. If you identify a range where you think the price of the underlying asset will move in the coming weeks, you can sell the Bear Call when the price is near resistance and the Bull Put spread when the price is near support. This way, you will collect higher premiums from the strategy.

A very important aspect of all options strategies is implied volatility. In the Short Iron Condor, the ideal situation is to have high implied volatility but declining from its peak. This applies to both the individual instrument and the VIX. For discussions on the VIX and all related considerations, I refer you to Chapter 17.

Options tend to have a fair price in low volatility contexts. Consequently, if you happen to be short, you probably will not earn much, as the premiums you collect from selling an option will not be high. When volatility increases, an amount is added to their prices, causing premiums to rise.

You have seen that Theta decreases rapidly as the expiration date approaches 30 days; having Theta on your side is crucial. Theta is what ensures you collect a high premium when selling the two options, Call and Put, significantly decreasing over time. A good way to do this is to select underlying assets with high Theta. Try to steer clear of underlying assets that have special situations, like legal troubles, earnings announcements, and other issues, as you want volatility to decrease during the operation, not increase.

At this point, you might be thinking: if time decay is in my favour and increases as the expiration approaches, why not trade weekly options? The answer lies in another Greek, **Gamma**. Gamma is the measure of the change in an option's Delta value with respect to a one-point change in the price of the underlying asset. That is, how much the Delta rises or falls with a 1% change in the underlying asset.

When it comes to Short Iron Condors, since they are almost always Theta positive (thus benefiting from time decay), they are also almost always Gamma negative (negatively influenced by an increase in Gamma). Gamma remains relatively flat until there are more than 15 days to expiration, below which it increases. This is a problem if your strikes are near the money because your options become increasingly sensitive to price changes. Your long strikes can no longer offset the price decreases of the short strikes, and the operation quickly becomes losing.

This is a significant issue for weekly options due to the Gamma risk and very limited adjustment period. This means that when entering into a Short Iron Condor, the sweet spot is between 30-45 days to expiration. Avoid speculating on options with only a week left until expiration or those with less than 30 days. Theta accelerates during this timeframe, causing premiums to decrease exponentially.

If you are new to options, you are taking on additional risk without being adequately compensated for that risk. It might seem enticing to make a profit for just a week's work, but this is certainly not a stable way to earn in the long run. Not to mention that commissions accumulate over time due to the increased number of trades, significantly reducing your returns.

You also need to keep an eye on another Greek: **Vega**. Vega measures how much an option's premium changes in response to a change in implied volatility. When implied volatility increases, Vega rises; when implied volatility decreases, Vega decreases.

In the Short Iron Condor, the ideal situation is for Vega to remain unchanged or decrease throughout the operation. The only exception is if the price of the underlying asset approaches the two purchased strikes. In these cases, higher volatility is positive because it implies a greater chance that the price will return to the range between the two sold strikes.

When selecting the strikes of the two options to sell, the Call and the Put, there is an important consideration to make. As I have mentioned, you need to sell the Call above a resistance level and the Put below a support level. But that is not all; you also need to consider the Delta. You have seen in the credit spread (Bear Call and Bull Put) that it is ideal to sell an option with a Delta not exceeding 20. With the Short Iron Condor, you have two credit spreads sold; choosing a Delta of 20 means your odds of success for the operation are 60%, which is not an enticing percentage.

This is because, with a Delta of 20, you have an 80% chance that at expiration, the price of the underlying asset will be below the strike of the sold Call and an 80% chance it will be above the strike of the sold Put. So, overall, the operation has a 60% chance of being successful. For this reason, my advice is to choose an option with a Delta of 10; this way, you will have 80% odds of success for the operation. With a Delta of 10, premiums will certainly be lower, but do not forget that the strategy allows you to cash in on two premiums, not just one.

Also important is the [choice of the underlying asset](#) to use in your strategy. ETFs on indices, such as SPY, QQQQ, etc., are certainly suitable for the Short Iron Condor because they are calmer instruments, with generally not too high volatility and are highly liquid. Alternatively, you can also use futures, but I recommend them for more experienced traders; ETFs are more suitable for beginners. You can delve into more specific stocks, but there are some considerations to make in this case.

- **Capitalisation**: It is crucial to choose stocks from large companies. Smaller companies can be more easily influenced by institutional trading volumes, potentially leading to market manipulation. Opting for companies with high trading volumes minimises these fluctuations and increases the likelihood of them staying within their trading ranges. Additionally, they ensure high liquidity in the market. Without a reasonable level of liquidity, transaction costs may rise due to wider bid-ask spreads. Almost every major company has adequate trading volumes, so sticking to them ensures liquidity is never an issue.
- **Price**: The stock should have a reasonably high price; low-priced stocks are unsuitable because there are not enough strike prices to make a Short Iron Condor work effectively. You want the widest range of strike prices possible, and there simply is not enough space between a low price and zero to provide that. My recommendation is to choose stocks with a price above $50.
- **News**: There should be no recent negative news about the company or imminent earnings releases. As mentioned earlier, you want to avoid high-volatility events when selecting stocks. This means steering clear of any negative news, such as legal issues, or earnings announcements. This applies throughout the operation. The Short Iron Condor is a neutral strategy, so you cannot use it to speculate on news or earnings. These events are binary in nature, meaning the stock either goes up or down. It certainly will not remain sideways.

A general rule for selecting strikes is that the distance between the two options comprising the Short Call should be equal to the distance between the two options comprising the Bull Put. This creates a balanced Condor and will not cost you additional margins due to unequal spreads. The choice of strike levels also impacts your profit. How much do you want to earn each month from a trade? Since a trade will last at least this duration, you want to ensure the strikes align with your profit expectations. You also need to choose a relatively realistic profit as the price movement of the underlying asset must be able to generate that return.

Keep in mind that underlying assets do not all have the same characteristics. It is better to simulate before trading with real money as this allows you to understand how realistic your expectations are for different instruments. During simulation, try to set up as many Short Iron Condors on ETFs, futures, stocks as possible. This will give you an idea of how volatility and liquidity work within them and how much you can reasonably expect to earn.

Now, after all these discussions, after so much theory, let's get a bit more practical. I will show you some examples of Short Iron Condors.

Example #1

Following my analysis on Disney, I decide to sell a Short Iron Condor because I am convinced that in the coming weeks the stock will move within the range of $95-$115, as shown in the chart in Figure 30.

Figure 30 - Disney daily chart (Mexem.com)

So, I sell a Bull Put constructed by selling the Put option with a strike of $95 and expiration in 33 days, and buy the Put option with a strike of $90, same expiration, collecting a premium of $0.19. At the same time, I sell a Short Call constructed by selling the Call option with a strike of $115 and expiration in 33 days, and buy the Call option with a strike of $120, also with a 33-day expiration, collecting a premium of $0.30. The margin required by the broker for the Short Iron Condor is $430, resulting in an ROI of:

ROI = ($49 [$19 + $30] / $430) x 100 = 11.40%

The maximum loss occurs when the price of the underlying asset rises above the strike of the purchased Call option, i.e., $120, or falls below the strike of the purchased Put option, i.e., $90. In the example with Disney:

Maximum Loss = (($95 – $90) x 100) – $49 (premium collected) = $451

or

Maximum Loss = (($120 – $115) x 100) – $49 (premium collected) = $451

The maximum profit, being a credit strategy, is given by the premiums collected and occurs when the price of the underlying asset is between the two strike prices of the options sold:

Maximum Profit = $19 (Bull Put premium) + $30 (Bear Call premium) = $49

There are two break-even points, the lower one occurs when the price of the underlying asset is equal to the strike of the Put option sold minus the collected premium. The upper break-even occurs when the price of the underlying asset equals the strike of the Call option sold plus the collected premium. In the example with Disney:

Lower Break-even = $95 – $0.19 (Bull Put premium) = $94.81

Upper Break-even = $115 + $0.30 (Short Call premium) = $115.30

Example #2

The second example is with Apple, of which you can see the chart in Figure 31

Figure 31 - Apple daily chart (Mexem.com)

My forecast is that the stock in the coming weeks may move within a range between $165 (support) and $195 (resistance). Therefore, I sell a Short Iron Condor structured as follows. I sell a Bull Put constructed by selling the Put option with a strike of $165 and buying the Put option with a strike of $160. At the same time, I sell a Short Call constructed by selling the Call option with a strike of $195 and buying the Call option with a strike of $200. All four options have a 33-day expiration.

From selling the Bull Put, I collect a premium of $0.21, and from selling the Bear Call, I collect a premium of $0.60, totalling $0.81. The broker requires a margin of $410 for the entire operation, resulting in an ROI of:

ROI = ($81 [$21 + $60] / $410) x 100 = 19.76%

The maximum loss occurs when the price of the underlying asset rises above the strike of the purchased Call option, i.e., $200, or falls below the strike of the purchased Put option, i.e., $160. In the example with Apple:

Maximum Loss = (($165 – $160) x 100) – $81 (premium collected) = $419

or

Maximum Loss = (($200 – $195) x 100) – $81 (premium collected) = $419

The maximum profit, being a credit strategy, is given by the premiums collected and occurs when the price of the underlying asset is between the two strike prices of the options sold:

Maximum Profit = $21 (Bull Put premium) + $60 (Bear Call premium) = $81

There are two break-even points, the lower one occurs when the price of the underlying asset is equal to the strike of the Put option sold minus the collected premium. The upper break-even occurs when the price of the underlying asset equals the strike of the Call option sold plus the collected premium. In the example with Apple:

Lower Break-even = $165 – $0.21 (Bull Put premium) = $164.79

Upper Break-even = $195 + $0.60 (Short Call premium) = $195.60

Example #3

The third and final example concerns Microsoft. Graphically, I have identified a range between $390 (support) and $430 (resistance) where I believe the stock may move in the coming weeks. Therefore, I decide to sell a Short Iron Condor structured by selling a Bull Put, constructed selling the Put option with a strike of $390 and buying the Put option with a strike of $385. At the same time, I sell a Bear Call constructed by selling the Call option with a strike of $430 and buying the Call option with a strike of $435. All options have a 33-day expiration. You can see the chart in Figure 32.

The premium I collect from selling the Bull Put is $0.84, and from selling the Bear Call is $1.20, totalling $2.04. The broker requires a margin of $290 to sell the Short Iron Condor, resulting in an ROI for the entire operation of:

ROI = ($204 [$84 + $120] / $290) x 100 = 70.34%

Important. The ROI of this operation is much higher than the previous ones. The reason is the width of the range determined by the two options for sale, significantly smaller compared to the examples above, just below 10% of the stock price against about 20% in the previous examples. This is to make you understand that the wider the range, the lower the profit (but more likely). Conversely, the narrower the range, the greater the profit (but the lower the odds of success).

Figure 32 - Microsoft daily chart (Mexem.com)

The maximum loss occurs when the price of the underlying asset rises above the strike of the Call option purchased, i.e., $435, or falls below the strike of the Put option purchased, i.e., $385. In the example with Microsoft:

Maximum Loss = (($390 – $385) x 100) – $204 (premium collected) = $296

or

Maximum Loss = (($435 – $430) x 100) – $204 (premium collected) = $296

The maximum profit, being a credit strategy, is given by the premiums collected and occurs when the price of the underlying asset is between the two strike prices of the options sold:

Maximum Profit = $84 (Bull Put premium) + $120 (Bear Call premium) = $204

There are two break-even points, the lower one occurs when the price of the underlying asset is equal to the strike of the Put option sold minus the collected premium. The upper break-even occurs when the price of the underlying asset equals the strike of the Call option sold plus the collected premium. In the example with Microsoft:

Lower Break-even = $390 – $0.84 (Bull Put premium) = $389.16

Upper Break-even = $430 + $1.20 (Short Call premium) = $431.20

Now, I believe the strategy is quite clear. Do not be misled by a risk (maximum loss) far greater than the gain (premiums collected), this strategy is highly profitable with, as mentioned, a success probability of 85-90%.

Ultimately, markets spend most of their time within ranges, moving sideways rather than in trends. With the Short Iron Condor, if constructed well, you once again align yourself with the odds of success. However, there can be mistakes or sudden events that may lead the operation into a loss. In such cases, adjustments can be made, and in the next chapter, I will illustrate some of these adjustments.

Manage of a Short Iron Condor

CHAPTER 13

~

The ideal scenario for a Short Iron Condor is for the sold options to expire worthless, allowing you to keep the entire premium. This also saves you on expiration fees. However, while this is a great scenario, the fact is that 30-45 days is a long time during which many things can happen. Therefore, it is crucial to be prepared with adjustment strategies. Below, I present four strategies that address almost every scenario you might encounter.

Remember that adjustments involve additional costs compared to the initial trade and are unavoidable. This might seem problematic, but always consider that the cost of an adjustment is far less than that of a losing trade. However, do not fall into the trap of continuously adjusting your trade: just because it is possible does not mean it is always the right choice. Sometimes your analysis may be incorrect, and in those cases, it is better to close the trade and allocate the money elsewhere.

The principles behind adjustments are simple. Your main goals should be:

- Protecting your capital and profits, avoiding excessive risk;
- Preventing small losses from turning into significant ones;
- Being willing to accept losses and move on to another trade.

Strategy #1

This is not a true adjustment strategy but rather an approach that many traders fail to adopt. Markets will move against your trade for certain periods, and if you allow enough time, they usually rebound, bringing the trade back into profit. Discipline is key to staying calm in these situations. Although it is difficult to watch your loss-making position, you should not exit the position just because it is losing, especially if the initial conditions that led you to open that trade have not changed.

In the case of a Short Iron Condor, it is extremely important to determine exit points if the trade moves against you. Typically, the bought strikes are these limits: they are the points where you achieve the maximum loss on the trade. If you are new to Short Iron Condors, you should let the market fluctuate towards these strikes and take your maximum loss on the trade.

You might be tempted to exit before the underlying asset's price reaches one of the two bought strikes. However, as a novice trader, you might be prone to exit early and potentially miss out on the profit you could have gained by keeping the trade open. Therefore, it is better to stay put even though it seems you will incur the maximum loss.

There is a fine line between being disciplined and hoping that the market will reverse its trend. If the underlying asset's price is at the maximum loss level and there is not much time left to expiration, you need to exit the trade or adjust it using one of the other options presented below. Staying in the trade without adjustments and hoping for a market rebound to bring you into profit is not professional trading. Traders who behave this way usually cannot bear the thought of being wrong and do not accept losses. As I always say, if hope made money in trading, I would have married an old high school friend of mine named "Hope."

However, if there are still several days left and the initial conditions that led you to open the Short Iron Condor have not changed, then it is advisable to keep the trade open, perhaps considering some adjustments to the strategy. Therefore, the first step when a trade is losing is always to remain calm, study the situation, and determine whether it is better to close the trade and take the loss or adjust the strategy.

Strategy #2

If your trade is in a loss, it means that the market is moving in a certain direction. Since you have set up a market-neutral trade, one half of the trade will be in profit while the other will be in loss. Suppose the underlying asset has risen too much for your liking, and the Bull Put is in profit while the Bear Call is in loss. You can move the Bear Call to a higher level. This means you will incur a loss on that half of the trade (which will be about 50% of your maximum loss).

Keep in mind that when you adjust the trade in this way, you are expressing the belief that the market will eventually reverse in the opposite direction. For example, if you notice that prices are attempting to break out of a range and you adjust the Bear Call upwards, you are saying that the breakout might be false and that prices will spike up only to then return to the range or, at most, not exceed the new limit set by the Bear Call. These judgments must be supported by solid evidence and not just hope, otherwise, you revert to the issue discussed in Strategy #1. If your new analysis indicates that the price will likely continue to rise, it is better to close the trade and study a new strategy.

Always keep an eye on volumes. An increase in volume (in the case of a bullish or bearish breakout) is an indicator of growing pressure that will support the price. Volumes in ranges tend to be lower than when the underlying asset is trending, because directional traders cannot profit during these periods and are out of the market. Examine volumes when prices rise and fall within the range. If the movement is accompanied by increasing volumes, this indicates a high probability of the price breaking out of the range.

Let me illustrate the strategy with an example. Suppose you have a Short Iron Condor on a stock currently trading at $100, with the following strikes:

- Sell a Put strike $95;
- Buy a Put strike $90;
- Sell a Call strike $105;
- Buy a Call strike $110.

Imagine that the price of the underlying asset quickly rises to $104. The Bull Put is in profit, while the Bear Call is in loss. To reduce the risk, you decide to move the Bear Call higher.

Close the Original Bear Call:

- Buy back the Call sold strike $105 (incurring a loss on this position).
- Sell the Call bought strike $110 (partially offsetting the loss).

Open a new Bear Call with higher strikes:

- Sell a Call strike $110;
- Buy a Call strike $115.

This adjustment repositions your Bear Call, reducing the risk that the underlying asset's price will exceed the new breakeven level. In doing so, keep a couple of things in mind:

- You have accepted a loss on the original position, but you have also increased the likelihood of retaining the entire premium of the Short Iron Condor with the new positioning.
- Your analysis indicated that the breakout is not a false move and that the price may continue to rise in the coming days but not so much as to surpass the resistance set by the new Bear Call sold.

Strategy #3

This strategy is an alternative to the previous one. In Strategy #2, you moved the Bear Call higher because your analysis indicated that the breakout above the resistance level was not a false signal. Therefore, you positioned the new Bear Call above the next resistance level, which the underlying asset's price is unlikely to surpass before the options expire.

However, if your analysis indicates that the upward movement is a false breakout and that the price will likely return to the range defined by the Short Iron Condor but you are concerned about the imminent expiration, you can opt for a variation of Strategy #2. You can sell another Bull Put with strikes closer to the current price of the underlying asset. The premium collected will effectively raise the breakeven of the Bear Call, giving the strategy more room to work.

Here an example. Suppose you have a Short Iron Condor on a hypothetical stock currently trading at $100, with the following strikes:

- Sell a Put strike $95;
- Buy a Put strike $90;
- Sell a Call strike $105;
- Buy a Call strike $110.

Imagine the price of the underlying asset quickly rises to $104. The Bull Put is in profit, while the Bear Call is in loss. After your analysis, you decide that the upward movement is a false breakout and that the price will probably return to the original range of the Short Iron Condor. However, with the option expiry approaching and the price possibly remaining high for some time, you decide to adopt this strategy:

Sell a new Bull Put:

- Sell a new Put strike $102;
- Buy a new Put strike $97.

This new trade allows you to collect an additional premium, which raises the breakeven of the Bear Call, giving the strategy more room to work. Assume that:

- The premium for selling the Put strike $102 is **$1.50**;
- The cost for buying the Put strike $97 is **$0.50**;
- Therefore, the net premium collected is **$1.00**.

The additional net premium of $1.00 adds to the total initial premium collected for the Short Iron Condor, raising the breakeven level of the Bear Call. This means the underlying price can rise up to $1.00 above the previous Bear Call breakeven, covered by the premium collected from the new Bull Put sold.

This strategy offers an effective solution when you expect the movement of the underlying asset's price to be temporary and return to the original range but are concerned about the imminent option expiry. Selling a new Bull Put allows you to gain additional room for the Bear Call and provides an added safety margin, raising the breakeven and reducing potential risk. By using this variation, you can better manage trades and adapt to changing market conditions, improving the odds of success and reducing overall risk.

Strategy #4

It can happen that your construction of the Short Iron Condor is flawed. You might have misjudged the distance between the sold strikes (the range within which the price must lie at expiration) when setting up the trade. This occurs more often than you might think, especially when prices move in wide ranges at the end of a trend. On a daily chart, such ranges can last for months. During this period, prices will form smaller ranges within the larger range.

For example, if you zoom in too much on the chart, you might end up confusing the smaller range with the larger, more stable range for trading. Alternatively, you might decide, based on your risk appetite, to trade within the narrower internal range. In these scenarios, it is advisable to place the bought strikes far from the sold ones. This way, you will have ample room to "adjust" the sold options (and thus the two credit spreads) if it becomes necessary to widen the distance between them (and, consequently, the range).

Sometimes, prices can leap beyond the smaller range and explore the "boundaries" of the larger range. In this case, you can close the sold option that has gone ITM and sell it again at a higher strike. This will obviously incur a temporary loss on the sold option that you closed early, but the money can be recovered if the trade closes in your favour.

You can also decide to close both sold options, thereby reducing the temporary loss and redesigning the trade's range. The important thing is to ensure that you adjust the trade before the expiration date; otherwise, you will end up with an assigned option, which will significantly increase your costs.

Let me show you an example to better understand this strategy. In Figure 33, you can see the same chart of Disney, a few days later.

Figure 33 - Disney daily chart (Mexem.com)

Observing it on a wider scale, you'll notice that the price is within a range between $102.00 (support) and $108.00 (resistance). This range is within a larger one, as seen in the previous chapter, bounded by support at $95.00 and resistance at $115.00.

Depending on your characteristics, risk tolerance, and analysis, you can decide to sell a Short Iron Condor based on the wider range or the narrower internal range.

If you opt for the latter strategy, you should place the two purchased strikes far from the sold strikes, specifically below the support and above the resistance of the wider range.

Thus, the Short Iron Condor will be constructed as follows:

- Sell a Put strike $102;
- Buy a Put strike $92;
- Sell a Call strike $108;
- Buy a Call strike $118.

Imagine that the price of the underlying asset rapidly increases to $107. The Bull Put is profitable, while the Bear Call is at a loss. The price might move out of the narrower range and continue within the wider range, at least in the upper part. The construction of the Short Iron Condor gives you ample room to adjust the strategy:

Adjustment of the Bear Call:

- Buy back the old Call with a $108 strike (taking a loss on this position);
- Sell a new Call with a $115 strike (partially compensating for the loss)

This new operation allows you to close the sale of the $108 Call with a temporary loss, but if the analysis remains valid and correct, you can collect the entire premium if the underlying asset closes within the wider range, having positioned the new sold Call above the resistance.

There are various strategies to adjust a Short Iron Condor, but many of these are more suitable for experienced traders. The ones I have shown you are some of the simplest and most used adjustments that you can implement if the trade is generating losses. However, if you have correctly identified market conditions, you will notice that you will need to intervene only a few times. The Short Iron Condor has a high probability of success (around 85-90%) and, if used correctly, can generate a monthly income.

Before moving on to another option strategy, I want to clarify something. You are probably wondering, "If there is a Short Iron Condor, is there also a Long Iron Condor?" Exactly, there is. The Long Iron Condor involves buying a Bull Call and a Bear Put, betting on a breakout from a range or on an imminent movement, whether upwards or downwards.

This strategy can be productive in some cases, such as before earnings releases, but it requires some experience and a more in-depth knowledge of options. If it were that easy to apply the strategy every time a company releases earnings and make a profit, everyone would be millionaires. In reality, it is not that simple: there are many aspects to consider, one of which is certainly volatility.

Based on the purchase of two Vertical Spreads, the Long Iron Condor is a debit strategy, as you pay the premiums to set it up. You need to find the right balance between not opening the trade too early, so as not to compromise the strategy's requirements, and not opening it too late, to avoid paying much higher premiums due to the increase in volatility in the days leading up to the earnings release. This increase in volatility could erode much of the profit from the subsequent movement, if not cause a loss.

Therefore, the Long Iron Condor is not suitable for beginners, but for more experienced traders. The risk does not lie so much in the potential loss, being limited to the premiums paid, but in the lack of experience and knowledge of certain dynamics that could lead to a much lower percentage of profitable trades compared to the Short Iron Condor.

The secret to obtaining a monthly income with options is to work only with strategies that offer the best success rates, and credit spreads are among these.

COVERED CALL

CHAPTER 14

After having seen the Short Iron Condor, it is now time to show you the simplest, most effective, and among the most used strategies: the **Covered Call**.

The "Covered Call" is truly the simplest strategy you can build with options, requiring knowledge of just a few basic concepts (which you have already seen explained in the earlier chapters). It is a calm and straightforward way to generate consistent earnings every month. This strategy implies that you have the underlying asset in your portfolio and that, ideally, it is already yielding a profit.

The Covered Call strategy involves trading both the underlying asset and one or more Call option contracts. In exchange for the premium collected from selling the Call option, which provides earnings in sideways markets and limited protection in downward markets, the trader gives up the potential profit generated by the underlying asset above the option's strike price.

As you saw in Chapter 3, selling (naked) Call options is very risky as it could lead to losing more than your capital. In this case, you do not risk getting into trouble because the sale of the Call option is covered by the underlying asset you hold in your portfolio. Indeed, in the event of assignment, you will be able to sell the underlying asset to the buyer (having it in your portfolio) at the Call option's strike price.

This means there are zero risks of not having enough money to cover a potential assignment. The only situation where you could lose money is if you buy the underlying asset and then immediately see the option assigned. In this case, the underlying asset will not have had enough time to increase in value, and you will close the position at a loss. For this reason, at the beginning of the chapter, I wrote that "this strategy implies that you have the underlying asset in your portfolio and *that, ideally, it is already yielding a profit*".

However, this is a scenario that rarely materialises (since the Call is OTM) and is highly unlikely to ever happen to you.

Furthermore, since you are simultaneously long (purchasing the underlying asset) and short (selling the Call option) on the underlying asset, this means you will not incur additional commission or trading costs. The Covered Call is an investment strategy like buying a stock or a futures contract.

As I always emphasise, the simplest strategies often turn out to be the best and most used, and the Covered Call is an example of this. You should use it since the premium (the money) it generates allows you to reinvest it in other strategies. Increasing your investments without resorting to debt (leverage) is an excellent way to grow your wealth, and the Covered Call allows you to do exactly that.

Now, as with the previous strategies, let's look at the characteristics of the Covered Call.

<u>Strategy</u>: the Covered Call is a strategy divided into two legs (or parts) where you buy or hold an underlying asset and sell out-of-the-money (OTM) Call option on the same underlying asset.

So:

Leg 1 = LONG with the underlying asset

Leg 2 = SHORT with the Call option

<u>A clarification</u>. Your investment is in the underlying asset, the Covered Call is a consequence, it comes afterward. Therefore, your purchase of the underlying must have valid reasons derived from your analysis; you should not buy a stock or an ETF without logic, only to then apply this strategy. That would be the wrong way to use the Covered Call.

<u>The main purpose of the Covered Call is to monetise existing investments to obtain extra income</u>.

<u>Max Profit</u>: you can profit from the underlying asset only up to the strike of the option or options you have sold. The maximum gain is equal to the difference between the Call option's strike and the entry price of the underlying asset plus the premium collected. It is achieved when the price of the underlying asset is equal to the Call option's strike.

Max Profit = (Call strike - underlying asset entry price) x 100 + premium

<u>Max Loss</u>: the risk of a Covered Call comes from the underlying asset, which could decrease in price below the break-even. The maximum loss occurs when the price of the underlying asset is zero minus the premium collected from selling the Call option.

Max Loss = underlying asset entry price x number of contracts/shares - premium

<u>Break-even</u>: it is equal to the difference between the entry price of the underlying asset and the strike of the Call option.

Break-even = underlying asset entry price - premium

<u>Time Decay</u>: since the Call option is sold, it has a positive Theta, which means the price decreases as the expiration approaches. Therefore, the Covered Call gains from time erosion if other factors remain constant.

<u>Volatility</u>: the Call option sold has a negative Vega, an increase in volatility will lead to an increase in the price of the Call option and therefore damage the position. Conversely, the Covered Call will benefit from a decrease in volatility.

When you sell a Covered Call, the performance is as follows (Figure 34):

COVERED CALL

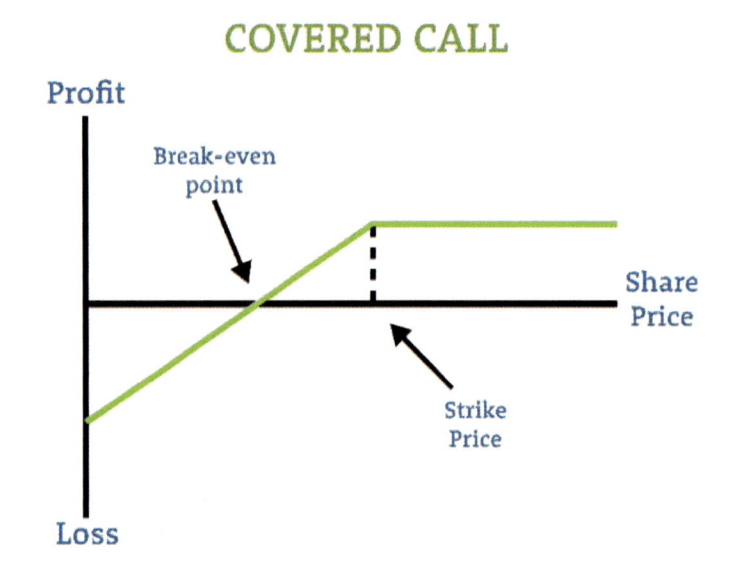

Figure 34 - Performance graph Short Iron Condor Covered Call

<u>To clarify</u>, the Covered Call strategy involves selling one or more Call options. Therefore, your position (i.e., options trade) will profit if the option price decreases, while it will lose as the price of the sold option increases.

If you are new to this, this strategy might initially seem contradictory. Let me explain further. You purchase an underlying asset; this means you have a bullish view of that market. Then, you sell a Call option, implying that you believe the underlying price will not surpass a certain level, thus going against your investment.

If you are also thinking this, you are not considering the time horizon of your investment and that of the Call option. Let me clarify. You bought an underlying asset because your analysis suggests that over the next 3, 5, or 10 years, the price will increase. However, during this period, the price will not always go up. There will be periods when it moves sideways or declines due to news or simple profit-taking. If there have not been changes in your analysis, you have no reason to sell the underlying asset and close the investment.

On the other hand, the Call option has a short-term time horizon and can be used to profit precisely during those periods when the underlying asset struggles to rise. So, during those times when you are not earning from the underlying asset, you will earn from selling a Call option.

Therefore, selling a Call option does not mean going against the investment made but rather capitalising on the pauses in the bullish trend and maximising the return on your investment.

Before delving into the strategy in more detail, there are still some aspects to consider. Which Call option strike should you sell? Which expiration date should you choose?

I will start with the choice of the strike. Which strike should you choose for the option sold? You need to consider a very important factor. If you are a short-term investor, the drop in extrinsic value must be balanced with the fact that you also want to ensure that your option ends ITM so that you can cash in both your profit on the underlying asset and the premium of the Call option.

So, to choose the right strike, you should rely on the Greeks. More precisely, on one of them: Delta. I have already explained what information it provides you. Delta, as mentioned, is a ratio that measures the price change of an option for a one-point change in the price of the underlying asset to which the option is linked. The ratio can have a positive value (between 1 and 0) or negative (between 0 and -1) depending on whether the option is a Call or a Put.

For example, a Call option on Netflix with a delta of 0.4 means that the option price will increase by 40 cents for a one-dollar increase in the price of Netflix stock. A Put option on Amazon with a delta of -0.25 means that the option price will decrease by 25 cents for a one-dollar increase in the price of Amazon stock (or increase by 25 cents for a one-dollar decrease in the price of Amazon stock).

You may come across Delta represented as a percentage; it does not change anything. A Delta of 40% is equivalent to 0.4; a Delta of -25% is equivalent to -0.25. It is just another way to represent the data.

Delta is a data point that can be predicted and is therefore very useful and often used by professional options portfolio managers. For a more in-depth explanation of Delta and the other Greeks, I refer you to Appendix A.

At this point, which Delta should you choose? Let me show you again a graph you have already seen in the Chapter 2 (Figure 35).

As you have already seen, options that lose the most value are those at-the-money (ATM). However, you cannot sell an ATM option because, as mentioned, your goal is not only to collect the premium but also to profit from the underlying asset. Therefore, the strike must be OTM but at the same time very close to ATM; we can set a rule for a strike with a delta around 0.4.

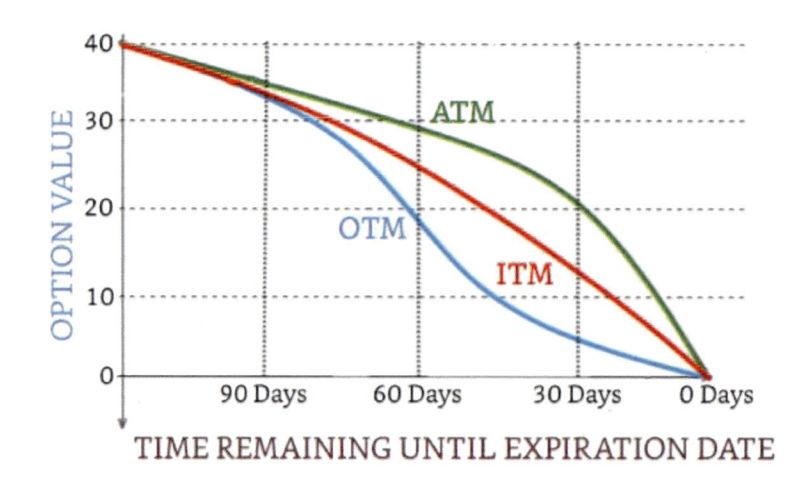

Figure 35 - Moneyness time decay

I will show you with an example using Apple, which at the time of writing this chapter is priced at 151.26. In Figure 36, you can see the options chain for Calls only.

BID x ASK	VOLUME	OPTN OPN I...	DELTA	GAMMA	VEGA	THETA	STRIKE
50.65 x 52.60	15	4.86K	0.994	0.001	0.010	-0.020	100
45.70 x 46.70	13	1.28K	0.992	0.001	0.010	-0.022	105
40.80 x 41.75	29	2.77K	0.987	0.001	0.016	-0.025	110
35.85 x 37.65	2	1.64K	0.982	0.002	0.024	-0.029	115
30.95 x 32.60	41	16.6K	0.972	0.003	0.034	-0.034	120
26.85 x 27.15	17	25.2K	0.956	0.005	0.049	-0.040	125
22.10 x 22.45	153	56.6K	0.929	0.008	0.069	-0.050	130
17.15 x 17.80	171	13.0K	0.882	0.013	0.090	-0.062	135
13.35 x 13.55	366	31.2K	0.811	0.018	0.132	-0.075	140
9.55 x 9.65	478	38.4K	0.706	0.024	0.154	-0.087	145
6.30 x 6.45	12.4K	77.2K	0.574	0.029	0.179	-0.090	150
3.80 x 3.90	3.64K	37.7K	0.423	0.031	0.178	-0.084	C 155
2.08 x 2.12	6.77K	44.3K	0.276	0.027	0.151	-0.068	160
1.04 x 1.05	4.84K	32.7K	0.160	0.020	0.110	-0.047	165
0.49 x 0.50	851	32.8K	0.085	0.013	0.067	-0.030	170
0.23 x 0.24	2.55K	18.2K	0.043	0.007	0.050	-0.018	175
0.12 x 0.13	182	17.6K	0.023	0.004	0.024	-0.011	180
0.06 x 0.08	597	12.1K	0.014	0.003	0.016	-0.007	185
0.02 x 0.08	198	20.8K	0.008	0.002	0.010	-0.005	190
0.02 x 0.04	2	8.80K	0.006	0.001	0.010	-0.004	195
0.03 x 0.05	60	31.1K	0.005	0.001	0.008	-0.004	200
0.01 x 0.06	1	2.46K	0.004	0.001	0.006	-0.003	205

Figure 36 - Apple options chain for Calls (Mexem.com)

Before proceeding, a couple of considerations. You can see that the $100 strike has a Delta of 0.994, which means that the probability of the option closing ITM is 99.4%. Given also the premium you will collect by selling this option, you might be tempted to do so. For a couple of good reasons, you should avoid this mistake: first, practically all the premium is intrinsic value; second, you will almost certainly be assigned and will have to sell the underlying at a price significantly lower than the current one. In conclusion, you will close the operation at a substantial break-even and will no longer have the investment (stocks) in your portfolio.

Selling the ATM strike is also not a smart thing to do. As mentioned, the price of Apple at the moment of writing is $151.26, so the ATM strike is $150. As already explained, you may not always be able to take the strike perfectly ATM; you will opt for the closest one. By selling the $150 strike, you will indeed collect a higher premium compared to, for example, the $155 strike, but you will get nothing from the underlying. On the contrary, in this case, you will incur a loss since you will sell the shares in the portfolio at $150 with a current price of $151.26.

Therefore, the choice should fall on OTM options and, as mentioned, on the strike with a Delta of approximately 0.4 (keep in mind that it will not always be possible to choose an option with a Delta of exactly 0.4; you will choose the one closest to this value). Highlighted in the figure above, the option to sell is the $155 strike. The Delta is 0.423, which means that the option has a probability of 42.3% of closing ITM.

If the option closes ITM, you will have a good chance of being assigned, closing the operation on the underlying with a profit of $3.74 per share in addition to receiving a premium of $3.80 per share from the sold Call option.

In summary:

- Purchase 100 shares of Apple at $151.26 for a total of $15,126.
- Shares assigned at $155 for a profit of $155 - $151.26 = $3.74 per share.
- Premium collected = $3.80 per share.
- Total profit = ($3.74 + $3.80) x 100 = $754.00 (minus commissions).
- ROI (Return on Investment) = 4.98%

Your profit once assigned is 4.98%, an excellent return considering that the sold Call option has a maturity of 33 days. Annualised, this percentage is 55.08% (slightly less considering the commissions on the purchase and sale of Apple shares), which helps you understand how, if executed correctly, this strategy can yield excellent profits.

That is, if you are a short-term investor. If, on the other hand, you are a long-term investor, your investment is the underlying asset purchased, and you have no interest in selling it following the assignment of the Call option (you will see assignment in Chapter 18). Therefore, the strike must be far enough from the underlying price so that the option expires OTM, and the underlying does not need to be sold to meet the assignment. At the same time, the strike must also have sufficient premium to give you a decent profit.

Your goal is to increase invested capital and obtain extra income (a premium) from the sold Call option. In this case, you should choose an option with a low Delta, close to zero. The choice should fall on the option with a Delta of approximately 0.05, meaning a 95% probability of the option expiring OTM.

Using the example of Apple again, you can see that the $175 strike has a Delta of 0.043, meaning the option has a 4.3% chance of closing ITM and you being assigned. The premium collected is $23, not much, but obtained monthly it allows you to earn $276 in a year, corresponding to an ROI of 1.82%. Considering that most brokers do not apply commissions to options that expire worthless, it is all net.

Sure, it is not a staggering percentage, but investing and speculating are two very different things, starting from the duration of the operation to the risk level. Here, your only risk is being assigned and forced to sell your Apple shares to fulfil your obligation. However, if this remote possibility (which I remind you is only 4.3%) were to occur, it would mean that Apple's price has risen to at least $175.

Given the current share price ($151.26), this would result in a price increase of at least $23.74 (i.e., a +15.69% increase in a maximum of 33 days). Not exactly a situation to tear your hair out over in despair. In these circumstances it is often the case after a strong rally, to see profit-taking that retraces the stock, giving the opportunity, if needed, to buy back the stock at a price lower than the one at which you were assigned.

The next choice to make is the expiration date of the Call option. Just like choosing the strike, deciding the expiration date of the option is equally fundamental for the success of this strategy. Choosing the wrong expiration date can lead to poor results.

To make the right choice, it is important to understand how option time decay occurs. As mentioned, you will choose an OTM option. The price of an OTM option, as I explained in Chapter 2, consists only of extrinsic value. The extrinsic value inherent in the price of an option is a measure of the probability that the option will go ITM.

The more time left until the option expires, the higher the probability that the option will be in the money.

Consequently, the extrinsic value of the option increases. So, on one hand, long-term options offer you great time value, but you also need to ensure that your option has a good chance of being assigned.

I will show you the time decay chart of an option again (Figure 37). As you can see, time decay is not linear; it accelerates once the option enters the last 30 days before expiration.

Therefore, whether you are a short-term or long-term investor, the expiration date of the Call option should be between 30 and 45 days. This will allow you both to have a greater chance of predicting the movement of the underlying asset and to collect a good premium thanks to the time value embedded in the option.

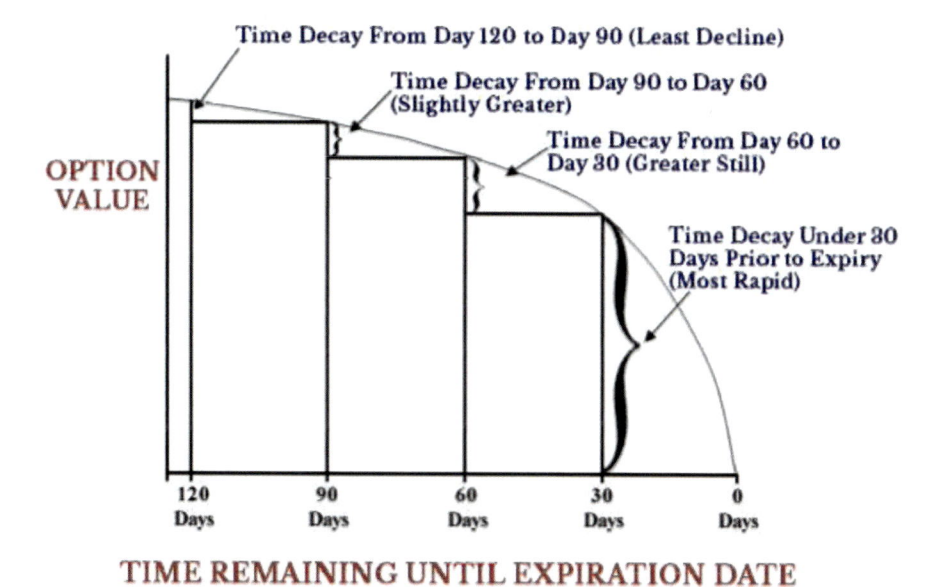

Figure 37 - Time Decay in an option

Now, to further clarify the strategy, I will show you another example before examining all the scenarios that can occur.

I have 100 Netflix shares in my portfolio (current price $612.81) and decide to use the Covered Call to generate monthly income, an additional gain on the investment. I have no intention of selling the underlying asset, the 100 Netflix shares, so the goal is for the sold Call option to expire OTM.

I open the options chain on Netflix with an expiration between 30 and 45 days (Figure 38) and choose a Call option with a Delta of about 0.05 (thus with a 95% probability of expiring OTM).

My choice falls on the Call option with a strike of $725, which has a Delta of 0.049 (thus a 4.9% chance of the option closing ITM), expiration in 33 days, a premium collected of $1.10 (average price) for an ROI of:

ROI = ($1.10 [premium collected] / $612.81 [initial stock price]) x 100 = 0.18%

The sale of the Call option is covered by my portfolio investment of 100 shares, so I will not pay any commission for the operation if the price exceeds the strike and I get assigned. Also, for the examples in this chapter, do not pay attention to the volumes as I took the screenshots shortly after the opening of Wall Street and therefore, generally, they are very low or absent.

This is the strategy, nothing complicated.

CALLS							STRIKE
BID x ASK	VOLUME	OPTN OPN I...	DELTA	GAMMA	VEGA	THETA	
4.15 x 4.35	15	278	0.155	0.004	0.520	-0.169	680
3.60 x 3.75	54	1.58K	0.137	0.004	0.521	-0.157	685
3.10 x 3.25	57	317	0.121	0.004	0.415	-0.142	690
2.66 x 2.76	27	123	0.107	0.003	0.419	-0.130	695
2.27 x 2.37	36	2.17K	0.094	0.003	0.366	-0.119	700
1.95 x 2.04	2	146	0.082	0.003	0.321	-0.107	705
1.66 x 1.75	3	220	0.072	0.002	0.324	-0.098	710
1.41 x 1.52	1	247	0.063	0.002	0.266	-0.088	715
1.20 x 1.31	1	156	0.055	0.002	0.238	-0.080	720
1.04 x 1.17		130	0.049	0.002	0.240	-0.072	725
0.90 x 1.02	3	216	0.043	0.002	0.213	-0.066	730
0.75 x 0.89		301	0.037	0.001	0.169	-0.059	735
0.65 x 0.78		222	0.033	0.001	0.170	-0.054	740
0.59 x 0.68		170	0.029	0.001	0.171	-0.048	745

Figure 38 - Netflix Call options chain (Mexem.com)

The ROI is not exceptional; annualised, it is a 2.16% extra gain ($1,320), but as mentioned, it is not speculation but practically zero-risk investment. Now, I will examine each of the four scenarios that can occur at the expiration of the Call option.

Scenario #1

Netflix moves sideways and, at the expiration date, has a value close to the stock purchase price. In this case, my portfolio remains almost unchanged as I gain little or nothing from the underlying asset (the stocks), but I collect the $110 premium from the sold Call option (which was the goal of the strategy).

Scenario #2

Netflix increases in price, and at the expiration date, it has a value between the stock purchase price and the strike of the sold Call option. In this case, my portfolio increases since the stocks have risen in price but not enough to send the Call option ITM, so I also collect the premium from the sold option (while keeping the stocks in the portfolio). This is the best-case scenario.

Scenario #3

Netflix increases significantly in price, and at the expiration date, it has a value above the strike ($725) of the sold Call option. In this case, I will be assigned, and I will have to use the stocks in the portfolio to fulfil my obligation.

However, as explained earlier, this is not necessarily a negative situation. The gain obtained with the underlying asset has exceeded my expectations, and as mentioned, I can wait for a retracement of the stock to re-enter at a price lower than the assignment price (which, however, is likely but not certain).

Scenario #4

Netflix decreases in price, and at the expiration date, it has a value lower than the current price at the time of selling the Covered Call ($612.81). In this case, I will have a decrease in my portfolio, having suffered a loss with the stocks that will be fully covered (if the decrease is less than $1.10) or partially covered (if the decrease is greater than $1.10) by the premium of the sold Call option.

In conclusion, there are two valid reasons to use the Covered Call. The first is because the strategy provides protection in case of a decline in the underlying asset's price. In the example above with Netflix, the collected premium of $1.10 per share reduces the breakeven point of holding the stocks and, therefore, reduces the risk.

However, the premium collected from selling a Covered Call is only a small fraction of the stock price, so the protection, if you do not use a stop-loss order on the underlying asset, is minimal.

The second reason is that selling a Covered Call generates additional income to the investment in the underlying asset. Many traders use the Covered Call for this reason. They have a regular selling program (usually monthly) of one or more Covered Calls with the goal of adding income to their annual returns.

You must keep in mind, however, that no strategy is without risk, and the Covered Call has some risks as well. In particular, there are two risks you encounter when using this strategy:

1. You may suffer a significant loss if the price of the underlying asset drops well below the breakeven point. In theory, if you do not put a stop-loss order on the underlying asset, the price can drop to zero.
2. You immediately give up the opportunity for a significant increase in the price of the underlying asset. The sold Call option, in fact, limits your maximum gain. In practice, by selling the option, you set a take profit on the underlying asset.

Before the final conclusions, I will provide some additional examples to explain in practice what has been explained, to clarify any doubts, if there are any.

Example #1

I am a fan of Elon Musk and I love Tesla, so I use the stock to generate monthly income through the Covered Call. I purchase Tesla at the current price of $172.70 and apply the strategy by selling a Call option with a Delta of about 0.40 with the goal of being assigned to collect the premium from the option sold and a capital gain on the underlying asset.

In Figure 39, you can see the Tesla Calls options chain.

BID x ASK	VOLUME	OPTN OPN I...	DELTA	GAMMA	VEGA	THETA	STRIKE
18.25 x 18.40	85	6.86K	0.735	0.013	0.196	-0.114	160
15.95 x 16.15	3	2.03K	0.689	0.014	0.216	-0.120	163.33
14.85 x 15.05	88	6.06K	0.664	0.014	0.218	-0.122	165
13.85 x 14.00	136	3.07K	0.639	0.015	0.219	-0.124	166.67
11.95 x 12.10	122	21.4K	0.588	0.016	0.232	-0.126	170
10.25 x 10.35	169	3.36K	0.535	0.016	0.235	-0.128	173.33
9.45 x 9.55	331	13.8K	0.508	0.016	0.237	-0.127	175
7.35 x 7.40	800	21.9K	0.430	0.016	0.233	-0.123	180
6.15 x 6.20	102	5.23K	0.381	0.015	0.218	-0.119	183.33
5.60 x 5.70	774	7.97K	0.357	0.015	0.220	-0.116	185

Figure 39 - Tesla Calls options chain (Mexem.com)

The choice falls on the $180 strike (my preference), with a 33-day expiration and a Delta of 0.430 (meaning the option has a 43% chance of closing ITM and me being assigned). The premium I collect from selling the option is $7.35 (BID price) for an ROI of:

ROI = ($7.35 [premium collected] / $172.70 [stock purchase price]) x 100 = 4.26%

In the event of assignment, then, in addition to the premium collected, I have a capital gain of $7.30 per share on the underlying asset ($180 strike at which I have been assigned minus $172.70 stock purchase price) for an overall trade ROI of:

Overall ROI = (($7.35 [premium collected] + $7.30 [capital gain]) / 172.70) x 100 = 8.48%

The annualised ROI is just over 93%, which clearly illustrates, if there was still any doubt, that this strategy is as simple as it is profitable (if used correctly).

Example #2

I have Amazon in my portfolio, and I absolutely do not want to part with it. Instead, I decide to sell Call options to further leverage my investment and at the same time generate a monthly income. The current price of Amazon is $189.86.

I open the options chain to decide which Call to sell (Figure 40).

BID x ASK	VOLUME	OPTN OPN I...	DELTA	GAMMA	VEGA	THETA	STRIKE
4.20 x 4.25	1.94K	16.0K	0.409	0.027	0.258	-0.077	195
3.30 x 3.35	32	4.39K	0.345	0.026	0.243	-0.071	197.5
2.55 x 2.57	1.03K	53.2K	0.285	0.024	0.220	-0.064	200
1.92 x 1.96	233	10.3K	0.231	0.021	0.191	-0.057	202.5
1.43 x 1.46	409	7.76K	0.184	0.019	0.179	-0.049	205
1.04 x 1.08	9	2.67K	0.142	0.016	0.163	-0.041	207.5
0.75 x 0.78	53	19.7K	0.109	0.013	0.131	-0.034	210
0.54 x 0.57	9	2.08K	0.083	0.011	0.100	-0.027	212.5
0.38 x 0.40	29	6.34K	0.062	0.009	0.080	-0.022	215
0.27 x 0.29	258	27.2K	0.046	0.007	0.075	-0.017	217.5
0.19 x 0.21	86	4.30K	0.034	0.005	0.053	-0.014	220

Figure 40 - Tesla Calls options chain (Mexem.com)

I need to look for an option to sell with a Delta as close to 0.05 as possible, given that, as mentioned, I do not intend to divest my investment in Amazon, and an expiration around 30 days. I choose the $217.50 strike (Delta of 0.046) with an expiration of 33 days. The premium collected is $0.28 (<u>average price</u>) for an ROI of:

ROI = ($0.28 [premium collected] / $189.86 [initial stock price]) x 100 = 0.15%

Annualised, the gain is about 1.80%, but if you consider that until a few years ago a bond investment yielded a similar percentage, and you get it without spending a penny, it is not to be disregarded.

Example #3

A stock I know well is Google, so I decide to use it in a Covered Call to generate a monthly profit. I purchase the stock at $170.82 and open the Calls options chain (Figure 41) to choose the one that best fits the strategy. Since I have no interest in keeping the stock in my portfolio, I want the option to expire ITM, so I will look for an option with a Delta close to 0.4 and an expiration of 30 days or slightly more.

CALLS							STRIKE
BID x ASK	VOLUME	OPTN OPN I...	DELTA	GAMMA	VEGA	THETA	
24.35 x 24.60	5	6.48K	0.939	0.007	0.075	-0.045	147.5
22.05 x 22.25	39	13.0K	0.922	0.009	0.086	-0.048	150
19.55 x 19.95	1	3.87K	0.902	0.011	0.111	-0.053	152.5
17.50 x 17.70	1.53K	11.3K	0.875	0.013	0.115	-0.057	155
15.35 x 15.50	1	7.66K	0.842	0.016	0.140	-0.062	157.5
13.20 x 13.45		14.0K	0.801	0.019	0.168	-0.067	160
11.30 x 11.50		2.91K	0.752	0.022	0.193	-0.071	162.5
9.50 x 9.65	59	14.2K	0.695	0.024	0.213	-0.075	165
6.40 x 6.50	115	7.18K	0.563	0.028	0.231	-0.078	170
4.05 x 4.10	86	9.47K	0.422	0.028	0.231	-0.073	175
2.37 x 2.41	141	37.9K	0.290	0.025	0.197	-0.061	180

Figure 41 - Google Calls options chain (Mexem.com)

The strike with a Delta close to 0.40 is $175 (Delta of 0.422), so I sell the option with a strike of $175, expiration in 33 days, with a collected premium of $4.05 (<u>BID price</u>) for an ROI of:

ROI = ($4.05 [premium collected] / $170.82 [stock purchase price]) x 100 = 2.37%

In case of assignment, in addition to the premium collected, I get a capital gain of $4.18 per share on the underlying asset ($175 strike at which I have been assigned minus $170.82 stock purchase price) for an overall trade ROI of:

Overall ROI = (($4.05 [premium collected] + $4.18 [capital gain]) / 170.82) x 100 = 4.82%

Obtaining 4.82% ROI every 33 days means achieving a 55% (about) increase in one year.

You can clearly see from these examples that the Covered Call is a very simple strategy, highly profitable, and with almost zero risk. The only difficulty, which lies with your analysis system, is choosing the right underlying asset. I have not provided any analysis of the stocks used in the examples in this chapter because it is not the focus of this book. It is up to you and your market analysis method to choose the right stock for the strategy.

In conclusion, there are periods, more or less extended, during an equity investment where there are no significant capital gains, the stock moves sideways, or even drops slightly. During these periods, you can decide to exploit this "apathy" of the stock and generate extra income from the market.

However, always keep in mind that if the stocks you own are not expected to rise soon and if you want to invest your money elsewhere, it is best to abandon the investment instead of trying to squeeze out some yield. The same applies if the initial conditions that led you to invest in a stock are no longer valid. Holding onto the stock could mean facing losses much larger than the income you will get from selling a Call option. This is something that many option traders working with Covered Calls overlook.

As much as the additional yield from selling a Call option may seem excellent, it pales in comparison to the gains from the underlying asset. The Call option can give you a premium of 4-5% in a month, but the underlying asset can do that in just one day. The downside is that these gains will remain "unrealised" until you close your investment in the underlying asset, which is why generating cash flow through Covered Calls is so valuable.

To complete the chapter, I will show you when it is advisable to close the strategy early to reopen a new one.

If the underlying asset drops or even just moves sideways, and your option has lost almost all of its value, and the expiration date is still far away, as you have seen with the vertical spread, it is worth buying back the sold Call option and selling a new one about a month later. It does not make sense to keep that option (and strategy) open for another ten days or two weeks just for a few dollars.

To put a rule in place, if the option price (which, I remind you, since it is OTM, is all extrinsic value, i.e., related to time decay) reaches 1% of the underlying asset price, then it is worthwhile to buy back the Call option and sell a new one with a longer expiration (about a month) and a new strike (never forget that the sold Call option must provide an acceptable premium).

The same goes if, a few days after selling the Call option, the price drops significantly due to a decline in the underlying asset. In this case, it is best to take home the gained profit immediately. Since you sold the Call option just a few days ago, you can sell a new one with a different strike, thereby achieving double profit with the same operation.

Essentially, you are leveraging time to your advantage, offering yourself more opportunities to make profitable trades.

If we want to establish a rule here as well, if in the first week the option price drops to 20% of the premium collected, then it is best to buy back the Call option and sell a new one with the same expiration but a new strike.

However, as already mentioned, but it is always good to repeat it several times, if you realise that your investment in the underlying asset is not going as expected or if the conditions that led you to buy it have changed, the wisest thing is to sell those stocks and allocate the money to a new investment. The silliest thing you can do is to keep holding onto the stock in the hope of making a bigger profit with options trading because it is extremely rare for option returns to offset the loss incurred with the underlying asset.

This is the Covered Call, a strategy that, if used correctly, will allow you to earn income every month (approximately) and generate a cash flow while, if you wish, keeping the investment in the underlying asset in your portfolio. It is a very simple strategy, with few rules, and low risk (almost exclusively related to the choice of the underlying asset to invest in).

The Covered Call is essentially risk-free because selling the option itself does not increase your risk profile. For this reason, it is an excellent strategy for beginners who understand market analysis but not yet options trading very well, and even though they make a mistake in choosing the option to sell, their only "problem" is that they will be forced to sell the underlying asset in their portfolio to fulfil their obligation (assumed when selling the Call option) as assigned. But as mentioned, this will be following a sharp rise in price, and the excellent capital gain obtained from the underlying asset will compensate for the disappointment of having to sell it.

Some Comments

Chapter 15

~

Once, after stating that I trade options, I was told that it is a form of gambling and that sooner or later I would lose my money. Options can indeed become extremely risky and dangerous, but it depends on the person using them. Those who have been trading options for over a decade will not find the more advanced strategies too complex. A trader who does not understand how Calls and Puts work will almost certainly fail to execute any strategy successfully. The secret lies in matching your skills, experience, and knowledge with the strategies that best suit your characteristics.

Statistics (though not publicly available) suggest that around 90% of traders blow up their accounts within a year of starting trading. With such a high failure rate, it is logical that options are considered risky. In fact, if you think about it, the stock market itself is considered risky because of these statistics. In reality, it is not the market or the instrument's fault if most traders lose their money, but simply due to the misuse of the tools at their disposal and lack of knowledge and experience.

The most common way most speculators operate with options is by using them as instruments to bet on price movements. If they think the underlying price is about to rise, they buy Call options; if they think it is about to fall, they buy Put options. What is certain is that none of these directional trades consistently perform well. Imagine if there were a way to short these traders' assets; you could make a lot of money.

This method exists, and that is where options strategies come into play. Since, as mentioned, most traders seek to buy options, what you need to do is sell them options. Most option buying trades fail because they end up expiring out of the money (OTM). So, by selling options, you align yourself with the side with the best odds of success.

This is the underlying thesis behind the Credit Spread, the Short Iron Condor, and the Covered Call. By selling options, you position yourself for success because the odds are in your favour from the start.

The ones I have presented in this book are just three of the many strategies that can be built with options; they are the simplest and lowest-risk ones. This is a text for beginners, so I will not delve into more complex and risky strategies like Strangle, Straddle, Calendar Spread, Diagonal Spread, Collar, or others. I leave it up to you, if you wish, once you have mastered the basics of options, to delve deeper into the subject.

However, you will find that the Credit Spread, the Short Iron Condor, and the Covered Call are among the most used and profitable strategies and are adept at exploiting all market conditions.

A temptation with options is to overly complicate them. By complexity, I mean using something that is not well understood. There are options strategies that involve many aspects, and if you do not understand the nuances of these aspects, you will inevitably incur losses. That is why I believe beginners should stick to simple options strategies, like the ones seen in this book. These strategies have few elements to keep track of and are based on simple rules for managing trades. They do not require much time to dedicate, without having to spend all day in front of a monitor watching charts. So, they are perfect for those who make options trading a part-time activity.

What makes options a unique tool is the ability to implement non-directional trading strategies. You have seen an example of this with the credit spread, where you can profit from declining or sideways-moving stock prices by simply leveraging time decay.

Options also allow you to take advantage of situations with unpredictable price movements. For example, if you anticipate a stock price will move significantly up or down, there are some options trading strategies that can help you set up a trade where you do not care about the direction but only the degree of price movement. These strategies are called volatility trading strategies.

In trading, volatility refers to the degree and strength of a price movement of an instrument. If a stock continually "jumps" with gap or often reverses, it is much more volatile than a stock that moves steadily without too many surprises. Investors view volatility as a "known unknown". They do not know which way prices will move, but they can assert with some degree of certainty that there will be a significant move in one of the two directions.

Volatility can help or harm them, and since they have no way to take advantage of it, they simply hold onto their portfolio investments. Options traders, on the other hand, can bet on certain obvious scenarios where volatility will be present in the market. For example, a significant announcement like earnings release will increase a stock's volatility even days before they are released. You might not know which way the market will move, but you know that volatility will increase. Some options strategies allow you to bet on volatility increasing or decreasing and to profit even though the underlying asset moves little or remains still. These strategies, as mentioned, require experience and a thorough understanding of all the dynamics surrounding options, so they are not suitable for beginners.

Options are misunderstood instruments, as they are often erroneously considered risky, even by experienced traders. This common belief harms many investors who choose to stand by when it comes to options, thus missing out on excellent opportunities. I am not suggesting you start trading options full-time, nor am I painting options as the Holy Grail, absolutely not. Instead, I recommend studying, understanding options, and integrating them into your investment strategy. You can use options, particularly the Covered Call, to generate steady income without exposing your account to additional risks, or the Credit Spread at the end of a retracement.

Many investors rely solely on capital gains from their investments. This is a mistake. It is a bit like buying a property and leaving it idle in the hope that it will increase in value over time and then reselling it. Experienced real estate investors immediately profit from their investment by renting it out. This way, they get a monthly cash flow, in addition to earning from capital gains.

However, many stock market investors do not follow this principle. Instead of trying to generate cash flows, they only worry about protecting their investments, often investing in gold and silver. Some even venture into alternative assets like cryptocurrencies. These may bring capital gains, but they do not provide any additional cash flow, something that can be done with low risk using options (and you have seen this with the Covered Call).

Options have another advantage, but if misunderstood, it can cause you problems and lead to significant losses: leverage. Leverage tends to attract two specific types of market participants. The first are people interested in easy profit schemes, often tending to greatly increase their exposure in the market through leverage, risking much more than their available capital. Of course, nothing and no one prevents you from risking more money than you can afford, but it is not very wise. These people are part of that famous 90% of traders who blow up their accounts within a year of starting trading, and options get a reputation for being risky.

The second type consists of people who understand the "philosophy" of leverage and use it wisely and correctly. They do not use leverage to increase their exposure in the market and therefore the risk. Instead, they use it as a way to use only a portion of the capital, allocating the remaining to other uses. This way, your risk remains unchanged, and you have more capital for other trades that, without leverage, you would not have been able to do.

Let's take a simple example. You have invested $40,000 in Amazon shares and do not want to close your investment and use that money in options trading. With leverage, you can use only 5-10% of that capital for options, leaving your Amazon investment almost intact.

This is another example of how everything in trading is dangerous if used incorrectly and becomes an opportunity for those who use it correctly. Options will not make you a million dollars in a day or make you rich in a few months. I leave these "shoots" to the numerous "gurus" on the internet with the rented Lamborghini. Options represent an excellent way to diversify your investments and to get a monthly income with limited risk as long as you use them correctly.

A question I often receive is: how much capital is needed to earn a salary? First of all, it depends on what you mean by salary: $1,000? $2,000? $5,000? Then we are not all the same (fortunately, otherwise, it would be so monotonous...), everyone has a different risk appetite. So even with the same capital available, two traders will most likely have two different trading approaches. However, one thing is certain: to earn certain amounts per month (I am always talking about averages), you need adequate capital. You cannot expect to make $5,000 per month with a capital of $2,000. You can try, but I assure you that you will have to increase the risk so much that sooner or later you will be wiped out of the market, losing all your money.

If we want to set a rule, to earn X dollars per month, you need to have capital of at least 15X dollars, that is, twenty times higher. So, for example, if you aim to earn a (average) monthly profit of $3,000, you need a capital of at least $45,000. Then it depends, as mentioned, on your risk appetite, which, if very low, can increase the amount. Always be wary of those who tell you that you can make good profits even with little money because they only care about their bank account and not people.

I hope this chapter has clarified some doubts. In the fourth part, you will see other aspects of options so that you have a clear and complete basic knowledge.

PART FOUR: MANAGEMENT

MONEY MANAGEMENT

CHAPTER 16

~

I want to make one thing clear to you right from the start: no one can tell you how you should manage your money. This is because we are all different people, and therefore different traders. So, if I were to tell you how you should manage your money, I would actually be telling you how I would manage that money, which is most likely not the right way for you.

However, I can give you guidelines to follow for managing your money and your trades, and that is part of a broader trading plan.

You have seen that the stop-loss must not be more than three times the premium collected when you sell a strategy. So, if you collect a premium of $100 from a strategy, the stop-loss must not exceed $300. This way, your maximum loss will be $200.

Once you learn this concept, you will have to determine how much a stop-loss can affect your account in percentage terms. In my experience, the stop-loss on a single trade should not exceed 1.5% to 2% of your capital (but you can decide on a different percentage), as shown below:

Capital	Maximum Stop-Loss
Capital < $20,000	Maximum stop-loss 2% of capital
Capital > $20,000	Maximum stop-loss 1.5% of capital

The stop-loss is useful for understanding which trades you can open and which ones it would be wiser to avoid. Let me give you an example. You have an account with $15,000 and you collect $220 from a Short Iron Condor. Following the rule, you set a stop-loss at three times the premium collected, which is $660.

- Premium collected: $220
- Stop-loss: $660 (three times the premium collected)
- Maximum tolerable loss: $300 (2% of the account)

So, your maximum loss will be:

Maximum loss = Stop-loss – Premium collected = $660 - $220 = $440

Your maximum loss ($440) exceeds your tolerable loss (2.93% instead of the 2%) that you have set for yourself. In this case, a solution could be to use slightly more OTM strikes in order to collect a smaller premium and have a stop-loss (and a maximum loss) lower than 2%.

Number of contracts. Moreover, thanks to the stop-loss, you also know how many option contracts you can trade. Here's an example. Suppose you have an account with $30,000 and you want to sell a Bull Put. For selling the strategy, you collect a premium of $75 per contract, so:

- Premium collected: $75
- Stop-loss per contract: $225 (three times the premium collected)
- Maximum loss per contract: $150 (stop-loss – premium collected = $225 - $75 = $150)
- Maximum tolerable loss per contract: $450 (1.5% of $30,000)
- Maximum number of contracts: 3 (maximum tolerable loss/maximum loss per contract = $450/$150 = 3).

What to do if a trade exceeds the maximum loss percentage?

The best solution is not to open that trade. Look for other opportunities that fit within your risk parameters. When I started trading (many years ago...), like many other traders, I had a small account and could not afford some trades, especially those with options on futures contracts. In the early years, I worked exclusively with US equities and ETFs.

As mentioned, the table above and the percentages can be modified according to your characteristics, feelings, risk appetite, and lifestyle. The important thing is that a trade does not stress you out; otherwise, you should review your money management because there is something wrong with it.

Minimum premium. How high does the minimum premium have to be for it to be worth collecting? I do not believe that there has to be a minimum dollar value, but that the proportion between the premium and the margin required by the broker should be taken into account. In other words, the ROI (Return on Investment).

As mentioned before, when working with options, you should aim to collect a premium of at least 4% per month. This translates to a minimum ROI of 4% (excluding Covered Calls). If the broker requires a margin of $500 for a Bull Put with a 2-month expiry, the premium collected must be at least $40 to achieve the goal of an 8% ROI over two months.

Strategies do not necessarily have to be closed at the expiry date. Let me show you another example in this regard. Imagine you have collected a premium of $80 (with an ROI of 12%) by selling a Bear Call with a 2-month expiry. After one month, you are earning $70 from the strategy.

- Premium collected: $80;
- Gain after one month: $70;

- ROI in one month: 10.5%.

Question? Do you want to keep the strategy open for another month?

The answer is obviously NO. In this case, it does not make sense to keep the strategy open for another month just to collect an additional $10 (1.5% ROI). Close the trade early to secure a profit of 10.5% in just one month and reuse the margin for a new trade that could give you a higher ROI.

You must also set a maximum loss on a monthly basis. In my opinion, if due to a series of negative events, you are losing 6%, then you should stop trading for that month, reflect on your mistakes, and wait for the negative period to end. So, in the case of a $10,000 account, the maximum monthly loss should not exceed $600 or at least the amount corresponding to the percentage you have decided on.

Risk/Reward. The last aspect concerning money management is the risk/return ratio. According to my experience and that of other good options traders before me, the ratio of the maximum loss (not the stop-loss, but the maximum risk) to the premium collected must not exceed 7: 1. So, if the premium is $80, the maximum risk must not exceed $560 (i.e., $80 x 7), that is, your Risk/Reward ratio must be a maximum of $560: $80.

Let me explain it better with an example. You sell a Bull Put on Apple built by selling a Put option with a strike price of $140 and buying a Put option with a strike price of $135, with an expiration date of April 21, '23. Thanks to this strategy, you collect a premium of $70. Doing the calculations, your maximum loss is given by:

Maximum Loss = ($140 - $135) x 100 - $70 (premium collected) = $430

In this case, the risk/return is approximately 6: 1, since $430/$70 = 6.14, and thus falls within your ratio.

Conclusions. While with equities these rules have to be followed to the letter, with ETFs and some futures (such as currencies) you can be a little more flexible because the movements are less profound. You will never see, for example, EUR-USD lose or gain 10% in a single day; this takes several weeks (barring special and rare events), so you have plenty of time to close or better manage your strategy.

On the contrary, with stocks that might gain or lose many percentage points as a result of news or earnings, these rules must always be applied.

You have to create your own rules for the best management of your money, protecting it from heavy losses that could not only eat into your account but also lead to a drop in confidence. Always remember that to trade in the financial markets, you need money. Your first thought must always be to protect your portfolio. You have to keep your risk under control at all times; you have to plan ahead.

In trading, there will always be trades closed at a loss. This is inevitable; perfection does not exist. You have to make sure that these losses do not cause you any problems.

People who fail to make money from trading blame the strategy and are always looking for new and more complicated ones (when simplicity in trading is the best way). They do not understand that the problem is not the strategy but themselves and their approach to the financial markets.

VOLATILITY AND VIX INDEX

CHAPTER 17

You have seen that volatility represents the change in the price of an underlying asset (stocks, futures, commodities, etc.) over a given period. Volatility indicates the market's nervousness about a particular underlying asset. The higher the volatility, the more nervous investors are, typically due to three possible reasons: news or rumours, reports or earnings, and panic selling.

Volatility is divided into implied volatility, which refers to future events, and historical volatility, which pertains to the past movements of the underlying asset. Therefore, it makes sense to sell options when volatility is higher (but not excessively so) because the premiums will undoubtedly be higher than when volatility is low.

This is because, with a more unpredictable market and consequently larger movements, the odds of the price of an underlying asset reaching the strike price of the written option will undoubtedly be more significant than when the underlying asset moves slowly. Thus, as always, greater risk means greater premium.

Volatility measures the magnitude of price movements that an underlying asset makes in a given period. The greater the price movements of that asset, the higher the level of volatility, and vice versa. Another important aspect of volatility is that, generally, when the price of an underlying asset rises, volatility decreases and vice versa; when an underlying asset declines, volatility increases.

An important indicator of volatility and a measure of market nervousness is the VIX. The VIX is a measure of the expectation of stock market volatility implied by options on the S&P 500 index; it is an indicator that measures the price traders are willing to pay to secure the right, but not the obligation, to invest up or down in the S&P 500.

Since you will primarily be working in the US market as far as options are concerned, you need to focus on protecting your trades from a sudden collapse or sharp rise in the underlying asset, particularly the stock market. The best way to protect yourself in these situations is the VIX. Volatility can be traded either with a futures contract, the VIX, or with an ETN (Exchange-Traded Note), the VXX. I will now analyse both to help you determine which of the two instruments is more suitable for your portfolio. In Figure 42, you can see the daily chart of the VIX; in Figure 43, the daily chart of the VXX.

Figure 42 - VIX futures daily chart (Mexem.com)

Figure 43 - VXX daily chart (Mexem.com)

The VIX is calculated in real-time by the Chicago Board Options Exchange (CBOE), and its chart is no different from that of any other market. However, it has significant peaks when the US market falls. Do not forget that the VIX moves inversely to the S&P 500 index. If the US index goes up, the VIX goes down, and vice versa. In contrast, the VXX chart tends towards zero. This means that if the US stock market does not move for a week, VXX still loses a few cents every day, whereas the futures contract remains relatively stable even when the market experiences minimal changes. Thus, the ETN, unlike the futures contract, always tends to decline.

Why is this? Because VXX is an ETN subject to expiry. As an ETN, VXX is backed by Barclay's credit rather than assets. VXX was launched with the ticker VXXB as "Series B" to replace the original VXX. The VXXB assumed the ticker VXX in May 2019. The old VXX was launched in January 2009 and expired in January 2019.

At first sight, it seems preferable to work with the futures contract rather than the ETN. However, the problem with the futures contract is that it has a much higher nominal value than the ETN. And what is the risk? The risk is that the "insurance" costs more than the asset to be protected. VIX futures are great, but only for those with highly capitalised trading accounts. For normal or small accounts, it is more convenient to work with ETN.

At this point, you need to determine how much to invest based on your risk capital, which I will explain in the next example. You have in your portfolio Bear Calls for $150 in premiums collected and Bull Puts for $1,300 in premiums collected. Let me start by saying that such a situation should never occur; your portfolio should never be unbalanced in one direction, regardless of the assets you are working with. In this case, if the market were to decline, you would have a loss of $2,600 (stop-loss) on the Bull Puts and a gain of $150 on the Bear Calls, resulting in a net loss of $2,450.

How can you protect yourself against a possible market drop that would be very negative for your portfolio? With a simple strategy that you can see in the table below:

Difference Between CALL Premiums and PUT Premiums	Investment to Cover Portfolio with VIX or VXX (Expiration Date: At Least 60 Days)
$1,000	$150

In the example above, you should invest $300 in the VIX (or VXX). In this way, if the index explodes, your $300 could become $1,500 or $2,000, if not more, in a few days, significantly recovering your loss on Bull Puts or even reducing it to zero. And if the market does not crash? All the better; it means you will take home all the premiums you collected from Bull Puts minus the $300 invested in "insurance".

Just as you do with car insurance, this is an excellent idea to protect yourself against movements negative for your positions (and your wallet). And if this insurance is lost, so much the better; it means that you have had no crashes, you have not harmed anyone, and, returning to options, you have worked well and taken home a profit.

A common point of confusion for beginner traders is the difference between implied volatility and the VIX. Implied volatility is one of many factors that go into the formula for determining the price of options. It is not something observable and is derived from the option's price. It measures the volatility of the underlying asset. Many traders automatically think that the VIX equals volatility.

This is partially true. The VIX is a futures contract that measures the implied volatility of the S&P 500. It is a measure of the implied volatility of the underlying market, not a single instrument. The two levels of volatility might not coincide. You might see high levels of VIX and low implied volatility on a specific stock. There is no simple way to address these scenarios. Usually, historically high implied volatility values negate the low levels of VIX.

As a general rule, the implied volatility of a single stock will dominate in the short term, but if your expiration date is more than 30 days away, then you should follow what the VIX indicates. When comparing implied volatility, one must look at the current values in relation to historical values.

What you saw above is just one example; there are many situations where it is better to hedge with the VIX or VXX. In trading, even a single piece of news overnight can overturn positions that were gaining just a few hours before. My advice is always to maintain a balanced and protected portfolio.

Figure 44 - S&P500 Index daily chart (Mexem.com)

I will now show you an example of how you can exploit volatility and thus the VIX index. Above, you can see the daily chart of the S&P 500 Index (Figure 44).

From 7 March to 13 March 2023, the index lost 5.21% in just three days. If it were treated as a stock, 5.21% is a significant movement, but not so rare to see. For an index, moreover the most capitalised in the world, this is a major drop that is uncommon to see in such a short time.

To better understand the situation, you need to shift your attention to the volatility index, the VIX (Figure 45).

Figure 45 - VIX Index daily chart (Mexem.com)

As you can see from the chart, during the same period, the VIX index increased by 50%, from a low of 19.0447 to a high of 28.6047, quite a significant difference indeed. And I assure you that this is minimal compared to deeper movements that the S&P 500 index can make, albeit rarely.

Clearly, such strong movements in such a short period are rare in the S&P 500. However, about a couple of times a year, the market tends to make major retracements, and volatility tends to make significant movements. To take advantage of these situations, it is therefore extremely convenient to periodically buy Call options on the VIX, especially during long periods of sideways or bullish market movement. This is for two reasons: firstly, to protect yourself against market declines, and secondly, to take advantage of cyclically occurring situations. Working with options means bringing statistics and probability to your side.

Options Assignment

CHAPTER 18

Options, besides being a speculative financial instrument, incorporate rights and obligations. There are a few important things to know.

When an individual sells, or writes, an option, they are accepting an obligation to sell the underlying asset at the strike price in the case of a Call option, or an obligation to buy the underlying asset in the case of a Put option.

An option assignment represents the seller's obligation to fulfil the terms of the contract by either selling or buying the underlying asset at the exercise price. This obligation is triggered when the buyer of an option contract exercises their right to buy or sell the underlying asset.

To ensure fairness in the distribution of American-style and European-style option assignments, the Options Clearing Corporation (OCC), which is the options industry clearinghouse, has an established process to randomly assign exercise notices to firms with accounts that have a short option position.

When a brokerage firm receives an assignment, it means that someone who has purchased an option has decided to exercise their right to buy (in the case of a Call option) or sell (in the case of a Put option) the underlying asset. The brokerage firm must then find a client (among its clients) who has sold (or written) an option of the same series (same type of option, same strike price, and same expiration date) and assign this client the obligation to fulfil the terms of the option.

The selection of the specific client who will receive the assignment can occur in two ways:

1. Randomly: the firm chooses a client at random from those who have a short option of the same series.
2. According to a specific procedure of the brokerage firm: the firm may have its own method for selecting the client, which could be based on criteria such as the time the position was opened, the size of the contract, or other factors determined by the firm's internal policy.

In both cases, the selected client must fulfil the obligations of the option, that is, sell or buy the underlying asset at the strike price established by the option contract.

While an option seller will always have some level of uncertainty, being assigned may be somewhat predictable. Only about 7% of options positions are typically exercised, but that does not imply that investors can expect to be assigned on only 7% of their short positions. Investors may have some, all, or none of their short positions assigned.

An investor who is assigned on a short option position is required to meet the terms of the written option contract upon receiving notification of the assignment. For example, in the case of a short equity Call, the seller of the option must deliver stock at the strike price and, in return, receives cash. An investor who does not already own the shares will need to acquire and deliver shares in return for cash in the amount of the strike price, multiplied by 100, since each contract represents 100 shares. In the case of a short equity Put, the seller of the option is required to purchase the stock at the strike price.

So, an assignment in options trading occurs when the seller (also known as the writer) of an options contract is obligated to fulfil their obligation to the buyer of the contract. This can occur in two different situations:

1. In the case of a Call option, the buyer of the contract has the right to purchase the underlying asset at a predetermined price (known as the strike price) at or before the expiration date of the option. If the buyer decides to exercise their right to buy the underlying asset, the seller of the option will be assigned, meaning they will have to sell the underlying asset to the buyer at the strike price.
2. In the case of a Put option, the buyer of the contract has the right to sell the underlying asset at a predetermined price (again, the strike price) at or before the expiration date of the option. If the buyer decides to exercise their right to sell the underlying asset, the seller of the option will be assigned, meaning they will have to buy the underlying asset from the buyer at the strike price.

It is important to note that in both cases, the seller of the option may be assigned at any time before the option's expiration date, depending on when the buyer decides to exercise their right to buy or sell the underlying asset. As a result, options sellers must be prepared to fulfil their obligations if they sell options contracts.

An important aspect to keep in mind is that the exercise of the option always takes place only after the markets close; therefore, the effects will only be seen on the first business day following the assignment, when the markets open.

It is necessary to distinguish the type of option. American and European options are two different types of options contracts that differ in the way they can be exercised.

- American Options: American options can be exercised at any time before the expiration date of the contract. This means that the buyer of an American option has the right to exercise their option at any time, including before the expiration date, which gives them more flexibility. For example, if a trader holds an American Call option and the price of the underlying asset increases significantly before the expiration date, they can exercise the option and take advantage of the price increase.

- [European Options]: European options, on the other hand, can only be exercised on the expiration date of the contract. This means that the buyer of a European option can only exercise their option on the expiration date, which can limit their flexibility. For example, if a trader holds a European Call option and the price of the underlying asset increases significantly before the expiration date, they cannot exercise the option and take advantage of the price increase until the expiration date.

Overall, American options are generally more valuable than European options because of their greater flexibility. This means that American options tend to have higher prices than European options with the same strike price and expiration date. However, there are some cases where European options may be more valuable, such as when the underlying asset does not pay any dividends. In such cases, the higher flexibility of American options may not be as valuable, and European options may be a better choice.

Another difference concerns the last day for buying and selling options. American-style options can be traded until the close of the expiration day. European-style options stop being traded the day before expiry.

The risk and reward are also different. European-style options have a lower risk because the expiration date is fixed and the loss or profit can be estimated. For this reason, the premiums are lower. In contrast, American-style options present a higher risk because the holder of an American-style option has the right to exercise the option at any time he or she sees fit. Consequently, the premiums are higher.

What happens if an investor opened a multi-leg strategy? When one leg is assigned, subsequent action may be required, which could include closing or adjusting the remaining position to avoid potential capital or margin implications resulting from the assignment. These actions may not be attractive and may result in a loss or a less-than-ideal gain.

I will now show you what it means in practice to be assigned. For example, suppose a trader sold a Call option on a stock with a strike price of $50, and the current price of the stock is $60. If the stock price increases to $70 before the expiration date, the buyer of the Call option may exercise their right to buy the stock at the lower strike price of $50. In this case, the seller will be assigned and must sell the stock to the buyer at $50, even though the stock price is now $70. As a result, the seller would experience a loss of $20 per share.

In summary, being assigned in options trading means that the seller must fulfil their obligation to the buyer of the options contract, even if it results in unexpected losses for the seller. Therefore, it is essential for options sellers to understand the potential risks involved and manage their positions accordingly.

Actually, the possibility of being assigned is quite rare and only concerns written options in any case. When you buy an option (Call or Put), you cannot be assigned, but you can choose to exercise your option.

As you have seen, the option price does not only have an intrinsic value. The option price (premium) is also determined by time (expiration date) and volatility. This makes it unreasonable for the buyer to exercise the option since the option premium is greater than the difference between the option strike and the price of the underlying asset. Therefore, assignment is more likely to occur on the expiration date or in the days immediately preceding it, when the option's extrinsic value is practically nil.

The writer of a Call or Put option has no control over the assignment, and it is impossible to know exactly when it might occur. As already mentioned, the risk of assignment becomes greater as the expiration date approaches, but this does not detract from the fact that assignment can occur at any time.

In conclusion, the probability of being assigned in options trading depends on various factors, such as the current price of the underlying asset, the strike price of the options contract, and the time until the options contract expiration. The probability of assignment may also vary depending on whether the option is an American or European style option.

For American options, the probability of assignment is generally higher than for European options because American options can be exercised at any time before the expiration date. Therefore, the probability of assignment for American options increases as the options contract gets closer to its expiration date.

For European options, the probability of assignment is lower than for American options because they can only be exercised on the expiration date. However, the probability of assignment can still occur if the options contract is in-the-money (meaning the strike price is favourable compared to the current price of the underlying asset) at the time of expiration.

To estimate the probability of being assigned, traders and investors can use various mathematical models and options pricing techniques, such as the Black-Scholes model. These models take into account various factors, such as the current market price of the underlying asset, the volatility of the asset, and the time to expiration, to estimate the likelihood of assignment.

Overall, the probability of being assigned in options trading depends on various factors, and traders should be aware of the potential risks and manage their positions accordingly.

Open Interest

CHAPTER 19

~

When analysing an underlying asset or an options strategy, it is crucial to seek as much confirmation as possible to make informed decisions. Market analysis requires discipline and hard work. However, this hard work can be incredibly fruitful when it allows you to put together the pieces of a complicated puzzle.

There are two important tools, volume and open interest, that I use in my analyses. They are essential technical metrics when it comes to understanding price direction. Let's first look at the difference between volume and open interest.

Volume

Volume in trading refers to the total number of shares, contracts, or units of a particular security that are traded within a given period of time. It is a crucial aspect of market analysis and provides valuable insights into the strength and liquidity of a security or market.

Key reasons why volume is important include:

a) **Market activity**: volume reflects the level of market activity and the intensity of buying and selling pressure. Higher volume indicates increased market interest and suggests that a large number of participants are actively buying or selling the security.

b) **Liquidity**: volume is closely related to liquidity, which refers to the ease with which a security can be bought or sold without causing significant price movement. Higher volume generally indicates higher liquidity, making it easier for traders to execute their orders without significantly impacting the security's price.

c) **Trend confirmation**: volume analysis can help confirm the validity of price trends. In an uptrend, higher volume during price advances and lower volume during price declines confirm the strength of the trend. Conversely, in a downtrend, higher volume during price declines and lower volume during price advances validate the bearish sentiment.

d) **Reversal signals**: significant changes in volume can indicate potential trend reversals. For example, a surge in volume accompanied by a sharp price decline could signal a trend reversal from bullish to bearish or vice versa. Traders often look for divergences between price and volume to identify potential turning points in the market.

Analysing volume patterns in conjunction with price patterns can provide valuable insights into market dynamics. For example, sudden surges in volume often indicate significant market events or news releases that attract a large number of traders. Volume spikes can provide insights into potential trend reversals, breakouts, or the initiation of new trends.

Also, the divergences that occur when the price and volume move in opposite directions, are very important. For example, if the price of a security is rising, but the volume is declining, it may suggest a weakening trend or lack of conviction from market participants.

So, the volume represents the real fight between supply and demand. It identifies an increase or decrease in interest of investors toward a particular market.

Open Interest

Open interest represents the total number of outstanding contracts held by market participants that have not been offset or closed out. It is a cumulative figure that fluctuates based on new positions created or existing positions liquidated. Key points about open interest include:

a) **Market participation**: open interest reflects the level of market participation and the number of active contracts in a specific derivative market. Higher open interest suggests greater market activity and interest from traders, while lower open interest may indicate reduced market participation.

b) **Liquidity**: open interest is closely linked to liquidity. Higher open interest generally implies higher liquidity, making it easier for you to enter or exit positions without significantly impacting prices. Adequate liquidity is essential for efficient trading and execution.

c) **Market sentiment**: analysing changes in open interest can provide insights into market sentiment. Rising open interest accompanied by price increases suggests bullish sentiment, as new positions are being created. Conversely, declining open interest coupled with price decreases may indicate bearish sentiment, as traders are closing out their positions.

d) **Support and resistance levels**: open interest levels can act as support or resistance levels for the underlying security or contract. High open interest at a specific price level may suggest that many market participants have vested interests at that level, making it a potential area of support or resistance.

Analysing open interest patterns can offer you valuable information. Here are some common interpretations:

a) **Increasing Open Interest**: When open interest rises, it indicates the creation of new positions in the market. This often occurs when traders have strong conviction about the direction of the market and are actively entering into new contracts. Increasing open interest can suggest the potential continuation of a trend.

b) **Decreasing Open Interest**: A decline in open interest implies the liquidation or closing out of positions. This could indicate that traders are unwinding their positions due to changing market conditions or reaching their profit targets. Decreasing open interest may suggest a potential reversal or a period of indecision in the market.

c) **High Open Interest with Price Consolidation**: when open interest remains high while prices consolidate within a narrow range, it could signify a build-up of potential energy in the market. You should interpret this as an impending breakout or a significant price move once the consolidation phase ends.

d) **Divergence with Price**: divergences between open interest and price can provide insights into market sentiment. For example, if prices are rising but open interest is declining, it may suggest that the current trend lacks conviction and could potentially reverse.

Let's see now better the significance of increasing open interest.

- Market Participation and Liquidity: increasing open interest indicates growing participation in options trading. As more traders and investors enter the market, the number of outstanding contracts increases, leading to higher liquidity. This liquidity benefits you by providing more opportunities to enter and exit positions at desirable prices with minimal slippage.
- Trading Activity and Sentiment: rising open interest suggests increased trading activity and reflects the sentiment of market participants. Higher open interest can indicate growing interest in a particular futures contract, security or options strategy. You should monitor changes in open interest to gauge market sentiment and potential shifts in supply and demand dynamics.
- Market Efficiency and Tightener Spreads: increasing open interest improves market efficiency. With more participants and trading activity, the bid-ask spreads tend to tighten, narrowing the gap between buying and selling prices. This results in more accurate pricing and reduced transaction costs for you.
- Trading Opportunities and Strategy Flexibility: higher open interest provides you with a broader range of trading opportunities and strategy flexibility. It enables the creation of more complex options strategies. Greater open interest also supports the availability of options with various strike prices and expiration dates, allowing you to tailor your positions to specific market expectations and risk profiles.
- Risk Management and Hedging: increasing open interest enhances your risk management capabilities. With a larger pool of contracts available, you can more effectively hedge your positions and manage risk exposure. Robust risk management

tools and strategies become more viable as open interest grows, enabling you to protect your portfolios from adverse price movements.

So, by monitoring changes in open interest, you can gain valuable insights into market sentiment and dynamics, allowing you to make more informed trading decisions. Ultimately, increasing open interest contributes to a more vibrant and robust options market, benefiting you, investors, and the overall financial ecosystem.

When open interest decreases, the opposite effects occur: market participation, liquidity, and trading opportunities diminish. Monitoring these changes can provide critical insights for making informed trading decisions. So, a decrease in open interest tends to have mostly negative implications and it would be wise not to use that underlying asset in your options trading and strategies.

Open interest is particularly relevant in options trading, as it represents the number of open option contracts. Traders analyse open interest in options to gauge the popularity of specific strike prices and expiration dates. Higher open interest in certain options may suggest that those levels are perceived as important by market participants, making them potential areas of support or resistance.

While open interest is a valuable tool for market analysis, it does have some limitations. It does not provide information about the direction of positions (long or short) or the motivations behind the trades. Additionally, open interest data alone may not be sufficient to make trading decisions. It should be used in conjunction with other technical indicators, fundamental analysis, and market sentiment for a comprehensive view.

Compared to futures, however, the open interest in options is more difficult to interpret. While with the C.O.T. report, the open interest in futures is divided into long (that is, contracts bought and still open) and short (contracts sold and still open), and therefore it is possible to understand which of the two parties prevails, in order to then make different considerations, something which is not possible with options.

In fact, in the options, it is possible to see the open interest for each strike of each expiry both for the Call and the Put. As well as the total (all strikes and expires) for the two types of options.

What cannot be determined is how many options have been bought and sold, how many are used to hedge purchases or sales of the underlying, how many are used in spread strategies and how many large traders there are (if any). However, you can also extrapolate some interesting data and make considerations that can help you in your analysis. Below, I show you some of them.

[The first data you get from the options open interest](#) is the following: the Put OTM strike of the nearest expiry with the highest open interest is an important support; the Call OTM strike of the closer expiry with the highest open interest is an important resistance.

I will demonstrate this with some examples. In Figure 46, you can see the gold options chain of both CALLS (left) and PUTS (right).

CALLS						STRIKE	PUTS						
BID x ASK	VOLUME OPTN OPN I...	DELTA	GAMMA	VEGA	THETA		BID x ASK	VOLUME OPTN OPN I...	DELTA	GAMMA	VEGA	THETA	IV: 12.4%
64.60 x 65.20	29	0.849	0.004	1.272	-0.329	1915	5.30 x 5.50	58	1.22K	-0.160	0.004	1.272	-0.337
60.40 x 61.10	86	0.829	0.004	1.274	-0.352	1920	6.00 x 6.30	37	285	-0.180	0.004	1.274	-0.360
56.30 x 57.00	393	0.807	0.005	1.419	-0.381	1925	7.00 x 7.30	128	3.13K	-0.202	0.005	1.419	-0.388
52.30 x 53.00	16	0.784	0.005	1.499	-0.402	1930	8.00 x 8.30	127	1.37K	-0.226	0.005	1.499	-0.409
48.50 x 49.20	34	0.758	0.005	1.501	-0.428	1935	9.20 x 9.50	125	1.10K	-0.252	0.005	1.502	-0.434
44.90 x 45.50	177	0.731	0.006	1.695	-0.450	1940	10.50 x 10.90	2.23K	2.88K	-0.278	0.006	1.695	-0.455
41.40 x 42.00	6 118	0.702	0.006	1.697	-0.471	1945	12.00 x 12.40	109	846	-0.308	0.006	1.698	-0.475
38.00 x 38.70	114 1.94K	0.672	0.006	1.791	-0.494	1950	13.70 x 14.00	637	5.17K	-0.338	0.006	1.792	-0.498
34.90 x 35.50	88	0.640	0.006	1.843	-0.508	1955	15.50 x 15.80	16	311	-0.369	0.006	1.844	-0.511
31.90 x 32.50	44 1.53K	0.608	0.007	1.845	-0.523	1960	17.40 x 17.70	24	1.86K	-0.402	0.007	1.846	-0.526
29.10 x 29.60	17 627	0.575	0.007	1.923	-0.533	1965	19.50 x 20.00	24	737	-0.434	0.007	1.924	-0.535
26.50 x 26.90	52 652	0.542	0.007	1.926	-0.539	1970	21.90 x 22.30	306	1.12K	-0.468	0.007	1.927	-0.541
24.00 x 24.40	58 1.93K	0.509	0.007	1.928	-0.547	1975	24.40 x 24.80	93	1.56K	-0.501	0.007	1.929	-0.548
21.70 x 22.10	94 1.14K	0.476	0.007	1.931	-0.543	1980	27.10 x 27.50	5	732	-0.534	0.007	1.931	-0.543
19.50 x 20.00	65 378	0.443	0.007	1.933	-0.544	1985	29.90 x 30.30		459	-0.566	0.007	1.934	-0.543
17.60 x 18.00	88 244	0.412	0.006	1.859	-0.536	1990	32.90 x 33.40	12	445	-0.598	0.007	1.860	-0.535
15.80 x 16.20	13 279	0.381	0.006	1.862	-0.526	1995	36.00 x 36.60		195	-0.629	0.006	1.863	-0.524
14.20 x 14.50	580 2.66K	0.351	0.006	1.837	-0.517	2000	39.40 x 40.00	25	1.67K	-0.659	0.006	1.837	-0.515
12.50 x 12.90	103 319	0.322	0.006	1.723	-0.498	2005	42.80 x 43.50		212	-0.688	0.006	1.724	-0.495
11.20 x 11.60	73 347	0.295	0.006	1.725	-0.483	2010	46.40 x 47.10	1	393	-0.715	0.006	1.725	-0.480
9.90 x 10.30	25 984	0.269	0.005	1.572	-0.465	2015	50.20 x 50.80		212	-0.741	0.005	1.572	-0.461
8.80 x 9.20	62 464	0.246	0.005	1.534	-0.444	2020	54.00 x 54.70		265	-0.765	0.005	1.534	-0.439
7.80 x 8.20	146 1.21K	0.223	0.005	1.535	-0.426	2025	58.00 x 58.70		1.35K	-0.787	0.005	1.534	-0.421
7.00 x 7.30	54 1.76K	0.202	0.005	1.328	-0.402	2030	62.10 x 62.80	1	338	-0.808	0.005	1.327	-0.397

Figure 46 - Gold options chain (Mexem.com)

Currently, the price of the gold futures contract is $1973. For Call OTM options, the highest open interest is at the 2000 strike (2.66K), while for Put OTM options, it is at the 1950 strike (5.17K). This indicates potential resistance at $2000 and support at $1950. Let us look at the chart of gold with the two levels of $1950 and $2000 highlighted (Figure 47).

Figure 47 - Gold daily chart (Mexem.com)

You can visually see how the price of gold has moved in recent weeks between the two levels identified with the open interest of the options and how in the past these two levels have acted as support or resistance depending on the moment.

Here is another example. In Figure 48 you can see the options chain on Block Inc., both CALLS (left) and PUTS (right).

Figure 48 - Block Inc. options chain (Mexem.com)

The current price of Block Inc. (SQ) is $63.60. The Call OTM options strike with the highest open interest is $70 (10.5K), while the Put OTM options strike with the highest open interest is $60 (11.4K).

In Figure 49 the Block Inc. chart with the two levels, $70 and $60, highlighted.

Figure 49 - Block Inc. daily chart (Mexem.com)

Even in this case, the price is not insensitive to the two levels identified with the options. Let's observe a final example before moving onto the reasons behind what you have seen. You can see in Figure 50 the options chain of the S&P futures, both CALLS (left) and PUTS (right).

Figure 50 - S&P futures options chain (Mexem.com)

Using the same procedure, the resistance is at $4400 (the Call OTM options strike with the highest open interest) and support is at $4200 (the Put OTM options strike with the highest open interest). In Figure 51, you can see the S&P futures chart.

Figure 51 - S&P futures daily chart (Mexem.com)

The reasoning behind what you have seen above is very simple. When you sell options, you always try to do so at levels that you think the price cannot break through. Most often you sell Call options on resistance (or above) and sell Put options on support (or below). The contracts you sell will focus on these levels.

However, do not think for a moment that these levels will not be overcome. You must always analyse the underlying correctly and follow the news, data, etc.

A [second aspect you can derive from the options open interest](#) is the following.

The further away a strike is from At-The-Money, the more open interest there will be in sold contracts. And vice versa. The closer a strike is to At-the-Money, the more its open interest will consist of contracts bought. This includes both those who are directional in the market and those who buy options to hedge an opposite position on an underlying asset.

Now, I guess you are thinking: if you take the ATM strike and subtract the open interest of the Put from that of the Call, you get a kind of net position of the C.O.T. report. Only in theory because the players are different. In the C.O.T. report, it is the Non-Commercial, i.e., hedge funds, investment banks, etc.; the open interest in options is mainly retail traders. So, the forces in the field are different.

Why do I mention this aspect? Precisely because the open interest in options is mainly made up of retail traders, it is visible to everyone and therefore the underlying asset can easily be manipulated against them.

I have had confirmation of this during my collaboration with a Swiss company that is involved in investments, especially in commodities. Working mainly with WTI crude oil, and also with EUR (the Euro futures), it was not uncommon to see on the day of the options expiry, the price close above a resistance or below a support. Actually, the whole week of the expiry of options is "nervous" due to the consequent increase in volatility as well.

This is visible in underlying assets with liquid options, such as WTI crude oil or gold, Amazon or Tesla. In those with low open interest, it is practically absent. Therefore, when working with certain stocks or commodities, pay attention to the expiration of the related options, there may be (for a few days at most) movements that do not reflect the fundamentals. In particular, if the price is close to a support or resistance.

I conclude this chapter that [concerns the open interest with a curiosity](#). Simply by reading the open interest of an underlying asset, you are able to understand if the price is in trend (bullish or bearish) or whether it is moving sideways (in a rectangular or triangular movement).

I am going to explain this better with a couple of examples. Below, you can see the first (Figure 52).

Figure 52 - Options chain (Mexem.com)

What you need to do is to observe the open interest of the In-The-Money Call and Put options. From the figure above, you can easily see that there are more Call ITM contracts than Put contracts.

It means that in the last days/weeks, the price of the underlying asset has increased (uptrend). Every time the At-The-Money strike price increased, the Call options purchased also increased. Meanwhile, those who had bought Put options at the same strike prices ended up closing trades at a loss, or otherwise rolling the position onto the next expiry.

Figure 53 - Apple daily futures chart (Mexem.com)

So, regarding the In-The-Money strike prices, when you see a high open interest in

Call options and low in Put ones, it means the underlying asset is in a bullish trend. Vice-versa, high open interest in Put ITM options and low in Call ones means the underlying asset is in a bearish trend.

The options chain above is that of Apple, and you can see the chart in Figure 53. The chart confirms what you read with the open interest, the uptrend of the underlying asset. Let's see a second example, below in Figure 54 the open interest.

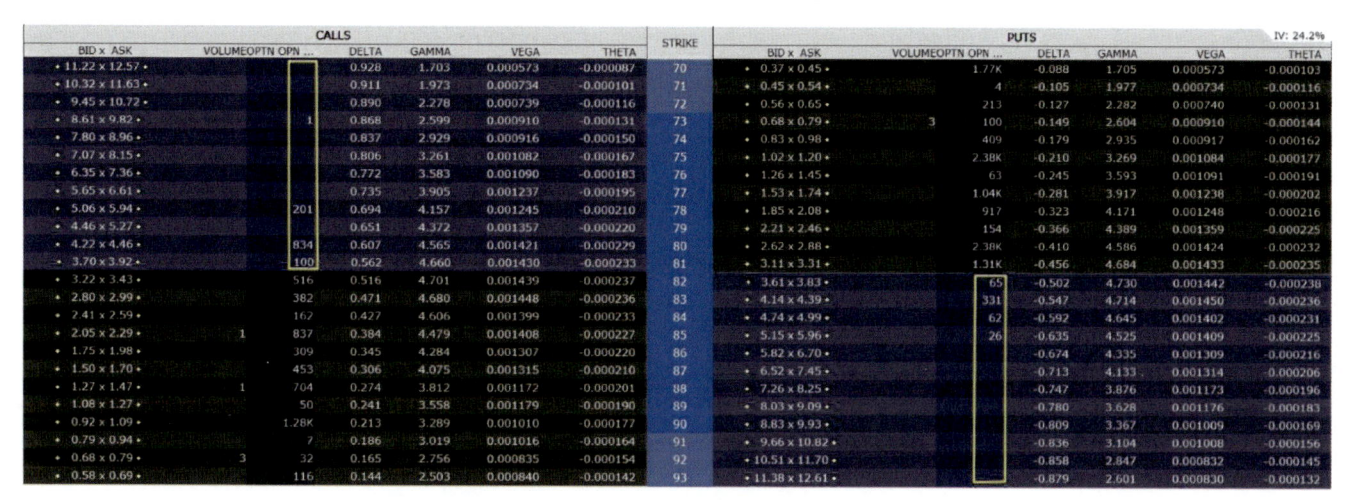

Figure 54 - Options chain (Mexem.com)

In this case, as regards In-The-Money options, you have a low open interest for both, Call and Put options. This means that the underlying asset is moving sideways, as shown in the chart in Figure 55.

Figure 55 - Cotton daily futures chart (Mexem.com)

Cotton is the underlying asset, and the above chart demonstrates how prices move within a range between $78 (support) and $88 (resistance).

In this case, if you were to see a substantial increase in the open interest in one of the two types of ITM options, it would mean that the price has finally taken a direction.

That's all about the open interest in options. I have provided you with additional information (and warning signs) that you can use in your analysis. The best advice I can give you is to use it differently from what you know with the C.O.T. In other words, use it as something that can be "hunted" by the strong hands.

Exploit the Acceleration

CHAPTER 20

The acceleration in options trading refers to an increase in the speed and intensity of trading activity in the options market. This phenomenon can manifest in various ways, such as through high trading volumes, rapid changes in options prices, or the use of advanced trading technologies. The primary cause of this acceleration is often a sudden increase in market volatility. When markets become more volatile, options prices tend to fluctuate rapidly, creating potential trading opportunities.

Significant events, such as earnings announcements, economic reports, mergers and acquisitions, economic crises or geopolitical developments, often lead to an increase in options volatility. During these periods of high volatility, trading opportunities increase significantly. Experienced traders can exploit these rapid price variations to enter and exit positions more effectively, maximising profits and minimising losses.

Moreover, the use of advanced technologies, such as trading algorithms and data analysis platforms, can significantly enhance a trader's ability to respond swiftly to market changes. These tools allow the identification of emerging trends and the execution of trades within fractions of a second, offering a substantial competitive advantage.

However, it is important to emphasise that the acceleration in options trading also involves high risks. While volatility can generate potential gains, it can also lead to rapid and substantial losses. For instance, a sudden drop in prices right after purchasing an option can quickly erode the value of the position. Therefore, it is essential to stay constantly informed about such events to avoid unpleasant surprises.

In options trading, there are various indicators, known as "Greeks," which numerically represent the different dimensions of risk associated with holding options. Among these, a significant parameter is Gamma. Gamma (γ) is a parameter that greatly influences the determination of options prices and is quite technical and difficult to comprehend. It measures the rate of change of an option's Delta with respect to the movement of the underlying asset.

Simply put, Gamma represents the acceleration of the option's price due to a sudden increase in the underlying asset's volatility. This acceleration leads to an increase in options prices well beyond their intrinsic value. Therefore, it is possible to trade by seeking to exploit Gamma, or the acceleration of the underlying asset's price, to obtain significantly higher premiums than those normally offered by the market due to a misalignment in the options pricing.

The relationship between Gamma and Delta can be visualised as follows:

- When an option is Out-The-Money or deeply In-The-Money, Gamma is relatively low and Delta changes more gradually.
- When an option is At-The-Money or Near-The-Money, Gamma is higher and Delta becomes more sensitive to price movements.

For a more in-depth understanding of Gamma and the other Greeks, refer to Appendix A.

Trading with Gamma requires extensive experience and knowledge of options dynamics, and therefore, it is not suitable for someone like you who is just starting out. However, the acceleration of the option's price (premium) is an important aspect you should be aware of, if only to understand how certain situations can be very risky and detrimental.

Now, to visually demonstrate what was explained above, I will show you a couple of examples of how an increase in the volatility of the underlying asset has led to a significant movement in the option. In Figure 56, you can see the daily chart of Alphabet Inc. (Google), and in Figure 57, the 8-hour chart of the ATM Call option with a strike price of 112.50 and an expiry in 44 days.

Figure 56 - Alphabet Inc. (Google) daily chart (Mexem.com)

Figure 57 - Alphabet Inc. (Google) option Call 112.50 8-hour chart (Mexem.com)

As you can see, Alphabet Inc. (Google), following positive earnings, opened sharply higher, reaching a peak of +5.36%. The ATM Call option with a strike price of 112.50 and an expiry of 44 days achieved a maximum performance of +93%.

The second example concerns Disney. In Figure 58, you can see the daily chart and in Figure 59, the 8-hour chart of the ATM Put option with a strike price of 100.

Figure 58 - Disney daily chart (Mexem.com)

Figure 59 - Disney option Put 100 8-hour chart (Mexem.com)

Disney, on the other hand, following disappointing earnings, opened sharply lower with a minimum of -9.36%. At the same time, the ATM Put option with a strike price of 100 and an expiry of 44 days reached a maximum of +131%.

Another example to show you how not only an increase in volatility but also its decrease affects option premiums. In Figure 60, you can see the Crude Oil chart, and in Figure 61, the chart of the ATM Call option with a strike price of $80 and 33 days to expiration.

Figure 60 - Crude Oil daily chart (Mexem.com)

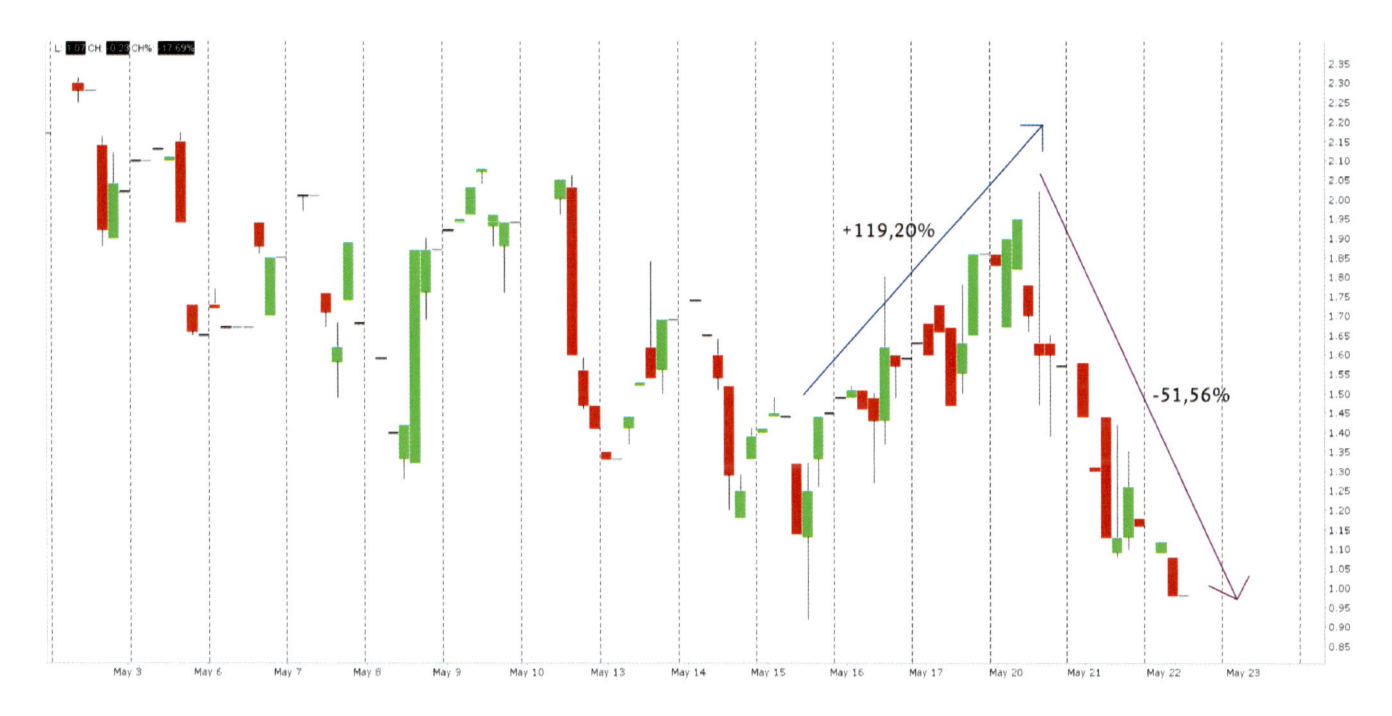

Figure 61 - Crude Oil 80 Call option 4-hour chart (Mexem.com)

From May 15 to May 20, the price of Crude Oil rose from a low of $76.24 to a high of $80.11, recording a gain of 5.08%. At the same time, the increase in Crude Oil price, coupled with a rise in volatility, led to a sharp acceleration in the Call option premium, which saw a performance of 119.57%.

Subsequently, from the high on May 20 to the low on May 21, Crude Oil experienced a loss of 2.63%, with a price still higher than the May 15 low. However, the Call option recorded a decline of 51.49%, returning to the minimum levels of May 15. This example clearly illustrates both the acceleration of the option premium when the underlying asset is strongly bought and the subsequent deceleration. When the buying halted and volatility collapsed, the Call option price also dropped significantly.

Had Crude Oil merely lateralised on May 21, with a price almost unchanged from the previous day, the Call option would still have lost a significant part of the previous days' gains. This example effectively explains the volatility and the acceleration/deceleration of options.

The beauty of options lies in the fact that their price (premium) can vary by 30-40% during a session, even with small movements in the underlying asset's price, due to the many variables influencing the price. A piece of advice I can give you is not to rush into opening a trade. It is better to make fewer trades but with a higher profit percentage.

For this reason, when I decide to sell a strategy, I set a price 20% higher than the current one, trying to take advantage of the daily movement of options. I assure you that this is something few traders do, but by the end of the year, it will result in several hundred dollars more in your account.

Having reached the end of the book, let me ask you a question: to take advantage of the Crude Oil rebound, would you have bought Call options or sold Put options? And once Crude Oil returned to the $80 area, would you have bought Put options or sold Call options?

If you have understood the thread of the book, you will already know the answer: sold Put options initially and sold Call options subsequently. This is for a very simple reason: the premium. To the premium is linked the risk, as you have seen:

Higher risk = Higher volatility = Higher premiums.

For example, buying a Put option once Crude Oil reached the $80 area would have exposed you to too many risks. Firstly, you would have paid a very high premium, inflated by volatility. Secondly, you would have made a profit only if Crude Oil had immediately reversed its trend. Even a brief lateralisation would have been enough to collapse volatility and significantly reduce the Put option's price, precluding you from making a profit. Just as an increase in volatility inflates option premiums, a decrease in volatility deflates them.

This chapter completes the discussion on options, providing you with a deep understanding of the dynamics that govern this market. Working with volatility and the acceleration or deceleration of option prices requires a certain level of experience, which you might currently lack. Therefore, I advise against pursuing this type of trading for now.

However, you now know that the price of an option can vary significantly compared to the underlying asset. For this reason, it is important to avoid underlying assets that, before the option's expiration, could present dynamics capable of increasing volatility.

At this point, you have learned the peculiarity of options: you can trade with the odds in your favour by selling strategies. This is the only way to achieve a consistent monthly income. Buying options involves too many uncertainties, from the right timing to the expiration date. This does not mean you cannot occasionally buy a Bull Call, but in the long run, this is not the way to achieve regular and steady gains over time.

Backtesting and Simulation

CHAPTER 21

~

Backtesting and simulation are essential tools for any options trader who wants to verify the effectiveness of their strategies before committing real capital. These processes allow traders to evaluate how a strategy would have performed in the past, helping to identify potential strengths and weaknesses. This chapter will explore the importance of backtesting and simulation, the methods for executing them, and how to interpret the results.

Backtesting

Let's start by defining backtesting. What is backtesting?

Backtesting is the practice of applying a trading strategy to historical data to assess how it would have performed in the past. This process is crucial for understanding the effectiveness of a strategy without risking real capital. By using past data, traders can simulate trades and observe the results they would have achieved if they had applied the strategy during that period. Here is a detailed look at what backtesting entails and why it is so important.

Now let's look at what the backtesting process involves.

1. Collecting Historical Data: The first phase of backtesting involves gathering accurate and complete historical data. This data includes the prices of underlying assets, option prices, trading volumes, and other relevant information. It is crucial that the data is of high quality, as inaccurate data can lead to misleading results.
2. Defining the Trading Strategy: Before performing backtesting, it is necessary to clearly define the trading strategy. This includes entry and exit criteria, risk management rules, and capital management. The strategy must be detailed so that it can be consistently applied to historical data.
3. Applying the Strategy to Historical Data: Using backtesting software, the strategy is applied to historical data. The software simulates trades as if they were executed during the specified time period. This includes buying and selling options, applying risk management rules, and continuously updating the portfolio.
4. Analysing the Results: Once backtesting is completed, the results are analysed to evaluate the performance of the strategy. This includes analysing metrics such as net profit,

maximum drawdown, the percentage of winning trades, and other performance measures. Analysing the results helps determine whether the strategy is valid and if it can be improved.

Understanding the importance of backtesting is fundamental for any options trader. Testing strategies on historical data offers a valuable opportunity to evaluate their effectiveness without risking real capital. Backtesting allows traders to simulate trades and analyse the results, providing a clear view of how the strategy would have performed under various market conditions. Backtesting is essential for:

1. Evaluating Effectiveness: Backtesting allows traders to evaluate the effectiveness of a strategy before using it in live trading. This helps to identify promising strategies and discard those that do not work.
2. Identifying Strengths and Weaknesses: By analysing backtesting results, traders can identify the strengths and weaknesses of their strategy. This enables them to make adjustments and improvements to optimise performance.
3. Reducing Risk: Testing a strategy on historical data helps reduce the risk associated with live trading. Traders can gain a better understanding of potential risks and rewards before committing real capital.
4. Building Confidence: Backtesting helps build confidence in the trading strategy. Knowing that a strategy has worked well in the past can give traders the confidence they need to follow it with discipline in real markets.
5. Optimising Strategies: Backtesting provides the opportunity to optimise trading strategies. Traders can test different variants of the strategy to see which one produces the best results.

Here is a practical example of backtesting. Suppose you want to test a Call option selling strategy on Microsoft. Here are the key steps:

- Collecting Historical Data: Gather historical data on Microsoft stock prices and related Call option prices for a five-year period.
- Defining the Strategy: Decide to sell a Call option with a strike price 5% above the current stock price each month (an invented strategy, do not follow this, it is just an example).
- Applying the Strategy: Use backtesting software to execute the strategy on the collected data, simulating trades month by month.
- Analysing the Results: Analyse net profit, maximum drawdown, and other performance metrics to determine the effectiveness of the strategy.

Below in Figures 62 and 63, you can see the tables with the results of the backtesting of this strategy.

Date	Price	Option_Strike	Option_Premium	Signal	Profit/Loss
2023-01-31	256.91	270	5	Sell Call	491.00
2023-02-28	249.42	262	5	Sell Call	2275.00
2023-03-31	272.17	286	5	Sell Call	-2310.00
2023-04-28	295.37	310	5	Sell Call	-1848.00
2023-05-31	313.85	330	5	Sell Call	-2126.00
2023-06-30	335.11	352	5	Sell Call	-1225.00
2023-07-31	347.36	365	5	Sell Call	1714.00
2023-08-31	330.22	347	5	Sell Call	514.00
2023-09-29	325.08	341	5	Sell Call	-702.00
2023-10-31	332.11	349	5	Sell Call	-614.00
2023-11-30	338.25	355	5	Sell Call	-600.00
2023-12-29	346.56	364	5	Sell Call	-1431.00

Figure 62 - Backtesting Strategy with Microsoft

Metric	Value
Total Profit	-6367.00
Max Drawdown	-2310.00
Winning Trades	3
Losing Trades	9
Winning Percentage	25.00%

Figure 63 - Performance of the Strategy with Microsoft

However, backtesting has some limitations:

- Curve Fitting: Over-optimising a strategy to fit historical data can lead to misleading results. It is important to avoid overfitting the strategy to past data, as this may not reflect future market conditions.
- Data Quality: Inaccurate or incomplete data can distort backtesting results. It is crucial to use high-quality data to obtain reliable results.
- Extraordinary Events: Unpredictable past events, such as financial crises or regulatory changes, may not reflect future market conditions. Backtesting results should be interpreted with these events in mind.

Backtesting is a powerful tool for any options trader. It allows traders to test, optimise, and validate strategies in a risk-free environment, reducing the likelihood of significant losses when transitioning to live trading. By implementing backtesting, traders can increase their confidence and likelihood of success in the options market.

Simulation

Simulation, or paper trading, is the process of testing a trading strategy in real time without committing real capital. This approach allows traders to apply their strategies in the current market, observing how they perform under present conditions. Unlike backtesting, which uses historical data to verify the performance of a strategy in the past, simulation occurs in the present. This allows traders to dynamically adapt to current market conditions and gain practical experience without financial risk.

Now let's look at what the simulation process involves:

1. Choosing the Platform: The first step in conducting an effective simulation is choosing a trading platform that offers paper trading capabilities. Many brokers and online trading platforms provide demo accounts that simulate real market conditions.
2. Defining the Strategy: As with backtesting, it is essential to have a well-defined trading strategy. This includes rules for entering and exiting trades, risk management, and capital allocation.
3. Executing Trades: Using the demo account, traders can execute trades based on their strategy, monitoring performance in real time. It is important to treat the simulation with the same seriousness as live trading to obtain meaningful results.
4. Monitoring and Analysis: During the simulation, traders must constantly monitor trades and analyse the results. This includes evaluating metrics such as net profit, drawdown, and the consistency of the strategy over time.

Here are the advantages of simulation:

1. Practical Experience: Simulation offers traders the opportunity to gain practical experience without risking money. This is particularly useful for beginners who are still learning the basics of trading.
2. Adaptation to Current Conditions: Since the simulation occurs in real time, traders can see how their strategies adapt to current market conditions. This helps identify any necessary adjustments to optimise performance.
3. Skill Improvement: Through simulation, traders can improve their trading skills, refining their ability to make quick and informed decisions.
4. Strategy Evaluation: Simulation allows traders to test and evaluate different trading strategies in a risk-free environment. This helps identify the most effective strategies to use in live trading.

Here is a practical example of simulation. Suppose you want to test a Call option buying strategy on Apple. Here is how to proceed:

- Choosing the Platform: Select a trading platform that offers paper trading.

- **Defining the Strategy**: Decide to buy a Call option with a strike price of $150 every time Apple stock price exceeds a 50-day moving average (again, this is purely invented for an example).
- **Executing Trades**: Use the demo account to execute the Call option buying trades every time the signal occurs and monitor the trade performance in real time.
- **Monitoring and Analysis**: Analyse the trade results, evaluating total profit, maximum drawdown, and other performance metrics to determine the effectiveness of the strategy.

Date	Price	50_MA	Option_Strike	Option_Premium	Signal	Next_Close	Profit/Loss
2023-01-10	143.07	135.86	150	10	Buy Call	144.98	188.00
2023-02-14	153.20	136.78	150	10	Buy Call	154.28	98.00
2023-03-03	156.30	137.56	150	10	Buy Call	158.92	252.00
2023-04-13	159.36	138.90	150	10	Buy Call	160.62	126.00
2023-05-15	164.30	140.45	150	10	Buy Call	165.88	148.00
2023-06-20	170.56	142.30	150	10	Buy Call	172.34	178.00
2023-07-25	174.88	144.60	150	10	Buy Call	175.89	91.00
2023-08-30	180.12	146.80	150	10	Buy Call	181.45	133.00
2023-09-15	185.40	148.90	150	10	Buy Call	186.50	110.00
2023-10-19	189.56	150.70	150	10	Buy Call	190.62	96.00
2023-11-24	193.87	152.45	150	10	Buy Call	195.38	151.00
2023-12-30	198.24	154.30	150	10	Buy Call	199.12	78.00

Figure 64 - Simulation Strategy with Apple

Metric	Value
Total Profit	1649.00
Max Drawdown	78.00
Winning Trades	12
Losing Trades	0
Winning Percentage	100%

Figure 65 - Performance of the Strategy with Apple

In Figures 64 and 65 above, you can see the tables with the results of the simulation of this strategy.

As with backtesting, simulation also has some limitations:

- Unrealistic Emotions: Since no real money is used, the emotions involved in live trading, such as fear and greed, may not be present. This can affect the evaluation of the strategy.
- Different Market Conditions: Even though the simulation occurs in real time, market conditions can change quickly. A strategy that works today might not work tomorrow.
- Platform Limitations: Some paper trading platforms may not perfectly replicate all real market conditions, such as liquidity and slippage. It is important to be aware of these limitations.

Simulation is a powerful tool for improving trading skills and testing strategies in a risk-free environment. It allows you to adapt to current market conditions, enhance your decision-making abilities, and evaluate the effectiveness of your strategies. By integrating simulation with backtesting, you can significantly increase your chances of success in the options market.

Now, to complete the chapter, here are some software options for backtesting and simulation. Unfortunately, they are in English and not always easy to understand. These are the paid ones.

1. **OptionNet Explorer (https://www.optionnetexplorer.com/)**

- Description: OptionNet Explorer is advanced software for backtesting and analysing options trading strategies. It provides comprehensive tools for position monitoring, risk analysis, and performance evaluation.
- Pros: Intuitive interface, detailed support for options, extensive backtesting features.
- Cons: Relatively high cost.

2. **Thinkorswim (https://www.schwab.com/trading/thinkorswim)**

- Description: Thinkorswim is a professional trading platform offered by TD Ameritrade with strong support for options trading, including advanced backtesting and simulation tools.
- Pros: Complete backtesting functionality for options, access to real-time market data, robust platform, paper trading capabilities.
- Cons: The learning curve can be steep for new users.

3. **ORATS (https://orats.com/)**

- Description: ORATS offers advanced tools for backtesting and analysing options strategies, with a particular focus on data quality and simulation accuracy.

- Pros: High-quality data, advanced analysis tools, excellent support for options strategies.
- Cons: Can be expensive for individual traders.

4. **eDeltaPro (https://www.edeltapro.com/)**

- Description: eDeltaPro is backtesting software specifically designed for options trading. It offers a wide range of tools for analysing options strategies and monitoring performance.
- Pros: Optimised for options trading, user-friendly interface, extensive backtesting features, trial period available.
- Cons: Less known compared to larger platforms.

5. **Cboe LiveVol (https://www.livevol.com/)**

- Description: LiveVol is a market analysis and backtesting platform offered by the Chicago Board Options Exchange (Cboe). It is particularly useful for options traders thanks to its detailed data and advanced analysis tools.
- Pros: Detailed options data, advanced analysis and backtesting tools, trial period available.
- Cons: Can be expensive and complex for new users.

Now the free software options, although less advanced (unless behind a subscription).

1. **TradingView (https://tradingview.com/)**

- Description: TradingView offers free technical analysis and backtesting tools. While advanced features require a paid subscription, the free version may be sufficient for beginners.
- Pros: Intuitive interface, wide range of technical indicators, support for custom scripts with Pine Script.
- Cons: Advanced backtesting features require a paid subscription.

2. **QuantConnect (https://www.quantconnect.com/)**

- Description: QuantConnect is an open-source platform offering advanced tools for backtesting and simulating trading strategies. It supports multiple programming languages, including Python and C#.
- Pros: Extensive library of historical data, support for multiple programming languages, active developer community.
- Cons: Requires programming knowledge.

3. **OptionStack (https://www.optionstack.com/)**

- Description: OptionStack offers a free platform for backtesting options strategies. While some advanced features require a paid subscription, the free version includes basic backtesting tools.
- Pros: Specific to options, free backtesting tools.
- Cons: Advanced features require a paid subscription.

4. **OpenBB Terminal (https://openbb.co/)**

- Description: OpenBB Terminal is a free and open-source platform offering financial analysis tools, including backtesting. It supports various asset classes, including options.
- Pros: Open-source, free, wide range of features.
- Cons: Requires programming knowledge, can be complex for beginners.

In conclusion, backtesting and simulation can help you understand if a strategy has been profitable and if it still is. Of course, they are not perfect and 100% reliable, as you have seen there are limitations to this type of "analysis". You also need to be good at inputting all the conditions of the strategy that must be met. However, it is an additional tool that can help you better understand all aspects, including the flaws and strengths of your strategy, even though it is not initially a simple topic for a novice.

This book has come to an end, now my final thoughts before the farewell.

Final Comments

Chapter 22

You have come to the end of this journey into the world of options. Before concluding, here are some thoughts starting with the take profit, a topic I have not treated so far. You have seen that you are not obliged to keep your options in the portfolio until the expiration date, but you can close your strategies earlier. This is not only in case the price hits your stop-loss but also if you get a satisfactory profit.

In the chapter on Money Management, you saw the case where you sell a strategy and are earning a good part of the premium, with the expiration date still far away. In this case, it is preferable to close the trade before the natural expiry.

For example, if a strategy has a 12% ROI with a 45-day expiration time and after only 15 days you are already earning 10%, it makes no sense to keep the strategy open for another month to earn only 2%, with the risk that the market will reverse and turn your +10% into a loss.

This is something to consider when managing your strategy because, once the trade is closed, the margin returns to your account and you can use it to open a new strategy and earn more money. This is especially important for those with small accounts.

You have also seen that when buying options, there is no absolute rule on stop-loss and target. However, on the rare occasions when I buy options, I try to close the trade as soon as possible because I do not like to be directional. As good as my analysis may be, I still do not know where the market will go; I just assumed it in my analysis, but even though I have the odds on my side, I basically do not know.

For example, I invest $150 (margin) in a Bull Call on Apple with the idea of making a profit of $250. If after one week there is a sharp increase in price and I have already made $100, I might decide to take the $100 home.

This is because when I buy options, my goal is not to make big gains, but I look at the percentage, and a $100 gain against a $150 investment represents a 66% ROI in one week.

Yes, I know. Speaking in absolute dollar terms, $100 in a week may seem like a paltry profit to you, but you have to think more professionally, that is, you have to look at your results as a percentage, and a 66% gain in a week is a great percentage and a great performance.

You are a beginner and initially, you most likely have a small account and work with one contract, but one day you will work with three, five, or ten contracts and that $100 will become $300, $500, or $1,000 per week, and I think you will agree with me that the result is no longer so paltry.

Another key aspect is time decay, which from being a "friend" when you sell options, becomes an "enemy" when you buy them. In particular, in the last 30 days, as you saw in Chapter 2, there is an acceleration. That is why when I buy options, I try to do so at least 90 days before the expiration date and close the trade at most 3 weeks before the expiration date. This is regardless of whether the trade has reached my target. So, when I buy options, I also have a time stop-loss.

If I followed the handbook, as Fontanills teaches, I would have to close the trade a little earlier, even four weeks before the expiration date. I still leave a little margin because I have seen that in reality, even between 30 and 20 days before the expiration date, there is still the opportunity to make profits. Instead, in the last 20 days, it becomes quite difficult.

Below, you can see the same chart seen in Chapter 2 with the Moneyness Time Decay (Figure 66).

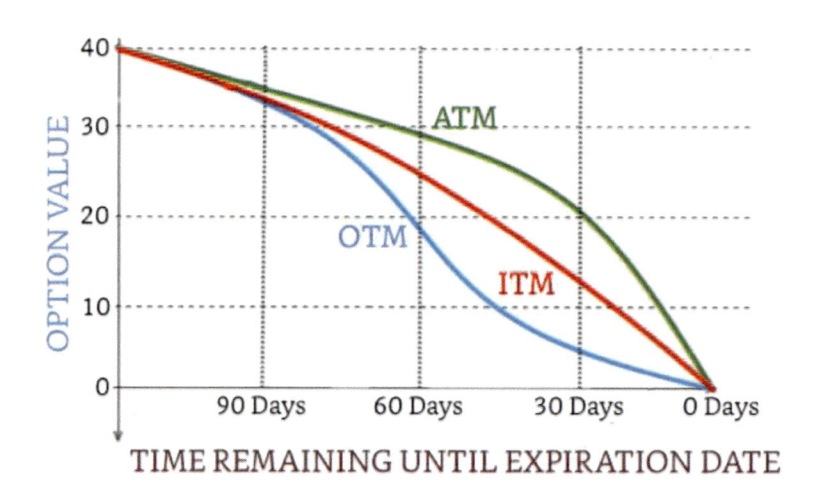

Figure 66 - Moneyness Time Decay

As you can see, when the expiration date is still a long way off, the option that loses the most value as the days go by is the OTM option, while the option that accelerates the price decline the most over the past month is clearly the ATM option. Therefore, if you buy/sell an option that has a strike price equal to or very close to the price of the underlying asset, you have to bear in mind that it is the one that will lose the most value in the last 20-30 days.

Two other aspects. Regarding the expiration date of options, we have different types, LEAPS, quarterly, monthly, and weekly. One of the questions I receive most often is:

which one is the best? What is the expiration date I should use?

The answer is always the same: it depends on you and your type of trading. If you work with a weekly option, you can get higher returns because the expiration date is closer, but you often have to stay nailed in front of the computer until Friday when the markets close.

This is because when selling options, the strike price of the written option often closes, on the expiration date, very close to the price of the underlying asset. Usually, the closer you get to the expiration date, the closer you sell strike prices close to the price of the underlying asset in order to obtain at least decent premiums.

Working with monthly or quarterly options, on the other hand, not only allows you to work with more liquid options but also allows you to manage your trades better, devoting much less time to options trading and thus reducing stress.

The use of one type of option rather than another also depends on your view of the underlying asset and the time horizon used in your analysis. In short, there is not one type of option that is better than another, but one type of option that is better suited to your trading and type of analysis.

The second aspect concerns how to receive exchange rate protection. With American options, the premiums collected are in US dollars. For American traders, there is no problem because they have an account in US dollars, their currency. But for those who are not American and who have, for example, a trading account in euros, Australian dollars, or British pounds, they will collect the gains (premiums) and losses of their options trades in American dollars.

It is clear that if during the year the exchange rate remains stable and moves within a certain range, it does not create any advantage or problem. The question arises if, over the course of the year, the exchange rate moves up or down by several percentage points, and this happens in every currency pair. For example, you can see the movement of the euro against the US dollar from January 2021 to September 2022 in which it lost 22.8%, or the subsequent rise of 16.3% from September 2022 to May 2023.

Important! An increase in the value of the dollar against your currency is positive if you have earned premiums, but negative if you have made losses. Conversely, a weakening of the dollar against your currency is negative if you have earned premiums, but positive if you have made losses.

The best solution is to manage the exchange rate to your advantage. For example, if you have a trading account in Canadian dollars and you have just cashed in 1000 US dollars in premiums, what should you do?

When trading with options, you have to look at the USD-CAD chart. If you think that the currency pair will increase in value in the coming days/weeks, it would be wise to keep your premiums collected in US dollars for a while longer. If, on the other hand, you think that USD-CAD will decrease in value in the coming days/weeks, then it is better to change them immediately into Canadian dollars.

If instead, you have a loss in US dollars and you think that the currency pair will increase in value in the next few days/weeks, then it is better to convert the lost US dollars into Canadian dollars immediately. If, on the other hand, you think that USD-CAD will decrease in value in the next few days/weeks, then it is better to still keep your loss in US dollars.

Personally, if I make a profit from my options strategies and then see it shrink by even 5% or 10% because of the euro-dollar exchange rate, I will not hide the fact that it really bothers me. I know traders with euro trading accounts who manage to increase their premium collected by 10-15% per year through careful management of the EUR-USD currency pair.

These latter aspects are very important and you must always take them into account. Options are so flexible that they allow you to create a very large number of strategies. Here you have seen only three, the simplest and most used, but there are many more. Even the Greeks are many more than you have seen. But this book is not meant to be a manual on options; if you need one, I recommend George Fontanills' book.

In all my books, you can learn my trading philosophy and this one on options is no exception. In trading, as in life, we must do simple things. Paulo Coelho said that: "the simple things are also the most extraordinary things, and only the wise can see them."

The best strategies are also the simplest. Many people believe that the reason for their failures in trading is due to the type of strategy. In reality, many of them are always looking for new and more complex strategies, without realizing that the problem is themselves.

Always remember that it is not how much you earn from trading, but how you do it that is important. Quality of life is more important than money. This concept always emerges in my books; this is how I trade.

For example, you should know that there is an options valuation model that applies a mathematical formula to calculate the theoretical value of an option based on a set of real variables. Many professional traders and options strategists rely on these models as an essential guide for evaluating their positions and managing risk.

However, no pricing model can reliably predict the behaviour of option prices. So why should I complicate my life and worry about the principles of theoretical options price?

With this book, I wanted to create a path to give you the basics, the knowledge you need to start navigating the options market. Practicing with a book is at least very difficult and doable. So, like everything else in trading, if you want to see a strategy in practice, you have to use the platform (the demo one, at least in the beginning) and when the markets are open. Only then can you perfect what you have learned and start creating your own experience.

This book is coming to an end; now, all you have to do is practice and gain experience. I understand that what I have tried to explain in the simplest possible way is actually a series of complicated concepts - at least, to begin with.

Do not worry, with time and application you will get used to having a complete and correct view of options trading. In this book, I have tried to convey all my experience. I hope I have succeeded at least in part and I hope that what you have read will help you to become an excellent options trader.

One last thing, at this point, many of you will have commented negatively whenever I mentioned the colours of the charts, "*it is a black and white book, how can I distinguish colours...*" You are absolutely right; the fact is that the same text is also available in the full-colour version, and I have not changed anything. However, to help you better understand the colours, I am sending the PDF with all the charts to anyone who requests it by emailing me at info@tradingwithdavid.com or using the form on the "Contact David" page of the site.

I conclude by thanking from the bottom of my heart Hannah for her efforts in proofreading this book into English, she was very kind and professional. You can contact her through her email: hannahhermes@gmail.com.

For any questions, my email is info@tradingwithdavid.com. On my website, https://tradingwithdavid.com you can find articles, analysis, books, and much more. You can find my other books on Amazon: https://amazon.com/author/davidcarli.

You can also follow me on:

- **Twitter**: https://twitter.com/tradingwdavid;
- **Instagram**: https://www.instagram.com/tradingwithdavidoriginal, with operational ideas and discussions of economics and financial markets;
- **YouTube**: https://www.youtube.com/channel/UCHB18Qsl0fm-eBULQEMsVSA;
- **TradingView**: https://www.tradingview.com/u/TradingwDavid.

Do not go yet; one last thing to do.

If you enjoyed this book or found it useful, I would be very grateful if you would post a short review on Amazon. Your support does make a difference, and I read all the reviews personally so I can get your feedback and make this book even better.

Thanks in advance for your support! I really hope that what you have read will help you in your trading.

Happy Trading to you all!

PART FIVE: APPENDIX

GREEKS

APPENDIX A

The Greeks are fundamental tools in options trading, as they allow the price of options to be defined comprehensively, not depending solely on the performance of the underlying asset. Paradoxically, thanks to the influence of the Greeks, an option can depreciate even if the underlying asset is gaining value in the market.

The Greeks numerically represent, in a synthetic and simple manner, the different dimensions of the risk associated with holding options, allowing us to evaluate and predict the variation in the option's price in relation to changes in the main external factors capable of influencing it: time, direction, and volatility.

There are many Greeks that we can use in options trading. Below you will find the four main and most important ones already discussed in this book.

Delta. Delta is one of the principal Greeks in options and is often considered the most important. It measures the change in the price of an option relative to the change in the price of the underlying asset. By analysing an option's Delta, we can get an idea of our potential gains or losses depending on the magnitude of the underlying asset's movement. Delta is represented by the Greek letter Δ and varies between -1 and +1 for individual options, depending on whether it is a Call or Put option.

More precisely:

- **Call Options**: Delta represents the change in the option's price for a $1 increase in the price of the underlying asset. A Call option with a Delta of 0.5, for example, indicates that the option's price will increase by $0.50 for every $1 increase in the underlying asset's price. The Delta for Call options typically range from 0 to 1.
- **Put Options**: Delta represents the change in the option's price for a $1 decrease in the price of the underlying asset. A Put option with a Delta of -0.5 means that the option's price will increase by $0.50 for every $1 decrease in the underlying asset's price. The Delta for Put options ranges from -1 to 0.

Depending on the option's strike price, Delta moves differently:

- **Out-of-the-Money (OTM)**: OTM options tend to have Deltas closer to 0.

Being far from being profitable, they have lower sensitivity to changes in the underlying asset's price.

- **At-the-Money (ATM)**: ATM options usually have a Delta around 0.5 for Calls and -0.5 for Puts. These options are more responsive to changes in the underlying asset's price.
- **In-the-Money (ITM)**: the Delta of an ITM option tends to be closer to 1 for Calls or -1 for Puts, indicating higher sensitivity to changes in the underlying asset's price.

Below, in Figure 67, you can see the relationship between Delta and Moneyness represented graphically.

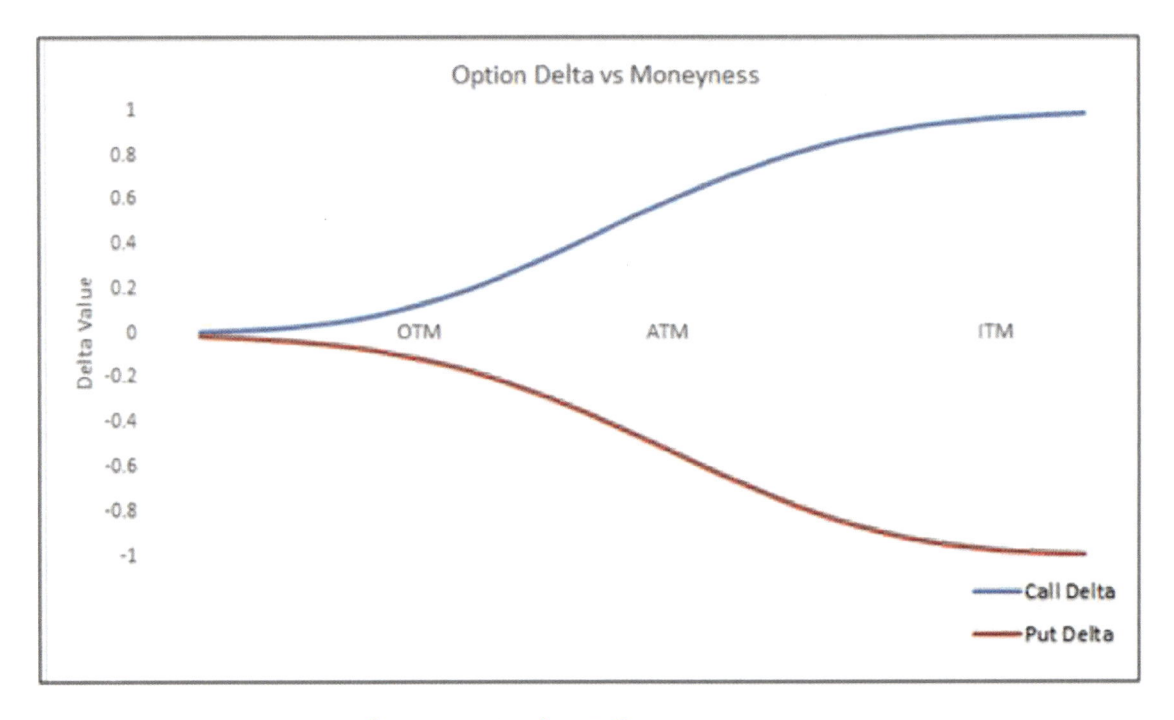

Figure 67 - Option Delta vs Moneyness

As you can see from the graph, the Delta of a Put option is exactly the mirror image of the Delta of a Call option.

Delta not only measures an option's sensitivity to changes in the price of the underlying asset but also serves as a hedge ratio for options traders. This unique feature allows traders to manage and mitigate risks associated with their options positions by creating a Delta-neutral portfolio.

I will show you an example to better illustrate the concept of Delta as a hedge ratio.

Suppose you hold a portfolio consisting of **400 shares** of a particular stock that is trading at **$100** per share. Concerned about downside risk in the stock market, you want to hedge your position against adverse price movements. The Delta of each ATM Put option is **-0.5**.

To create a Delta-neutral portfolio, you can use Delta as a guide to determine the number of ATM Put option contracts to purchase:

Number of Put options to buy = (Number of shares) / (Shares per contract) / (ATM Put option Delta)

Assuming each option contract represents 100 shares, the calculation would be:

Number of Put options to buy = 400 / 100 / -0.5 = 8

Therefore, to create a Delta-neutral portfolio, you would need to buy 8 ATM Put option contracts.

As verification, you know that a Put option with a Delta of -0.5 means that if the stock price drops by $1, the value of the option increases by $0.5. If the stock price drops by $1, the value of your Put options will increase by:

400 (shares) x -$1 = -$400

Conversely, your Put options will increase in value by:

$0,5 per contract x 8 contracts x 100 (number of shares per contract) = $400.

The Delta-neutral portfolio ensures that the overall Delta of your position is close to zero. This means you are not overly exposed to directional moves in the stock price. Whether the stock price goes up or down, the impact on your portfolio's value will be minimised, as the gains from the long Put options position will offset the losses in the underlying stocks and vice versa.

However, it is important to note that achieving a perfectly Delta-neutral position can be challenging due to factors such as transaction costs, bid-ask spreads, and the dynamic nature of Delta itself. Therefore, traders often aim to get as close to Delta-neutral as possible, rather than achieving an exact Delta-neutral state.

It should also be remembered that Delta is mathematically the first derivative of the option premium with respect to the underlying asset, so it is only reliable for small movements of the underlying. In theory, a Delta-neutral strategy requires constant efforts to maintain the right balance.

By using Delta as a hedge ratio, options traders can actively manage their risk exposure and protect their positions from adverse market movements. Delta-neutral strategies can be particularly useful when the trader anticipates uncertainty or volatility in the underlying asset's price.

Delta is a critical concept in options trading, providing insights into an option's sensitivity to changes in the underlying asset's price. Understanding Delta values and their interpretations allows options traders to make more informed decisions about strategy selection, risk management, and portfolio hedging.

Gamma. Gamma measures the rate of change of an option's Delta. It quantifies how sensitive the Delta of an option is to movements in the underlying asset's price. Gamma is defined as the Delta of the Delta, as it is mathematically the second derivative of the option's premium with respect to the underlying asset.

Gamma is represented by the Greek letter Γ, and its values can vary depending on whether the option is a Call or a Put, typically ranging from 0 to positive values.

- **Call Options**: Gamma represents the change in the option's Delta for every $1 change in the price of the underlying asset. A Call option with a Gamma of 0.05 indicates that the Delta of the option will increase by 0.05 for every $1 increase in the underlying asset's price. This means that Gamma measures the acceleration or deceleration of Delta changes in response to movements in the underlying asset's price.
- **Put Options**: Conversely, for Put options, Gamma represents the change in the option's Delta for every $1 change in the price of the underlying asset. A Put option with a Gamma of 0.03 means that the Delta of the option will increase by 0.03 for every $1 decrease in the underlying asset's price. Similar to Call options, Gamma for Puts measures the acceleration or deceleration of Delta changes but in response to decreases in the underlying asset's price.

Here is a practical example. A particular stock is currently trading at $100. The Call option with a two-month expiry and a strike price of $100 (At-the-Money) is quoted at $5, has a Delta of 0.50, and a Gamma of 0.10.

Imagine the stock price increases from $100 to $101. With this information, we can estimate the new Delta and the price of the Call option.

1. *Calculation of the new Delta*:

a) The initial Delta of the Call option is **0.50**.
b) The Gamma is **0.10**, which means that for every $1 increase in the price of the underlying asset, the Delta will increase by 0.10.
c) Therefore, if the stock price increases to $101, *the new Delta* will be:

New Δ (Delta) = Old Δ (Delta) + Γ (Gamma) = 0,50 + 0,10 = 0,60

2. *Estimate of the new option price*:

- Initially, the Call option is quoted at **$5**.
- With a Delta of **0.50**, a **$1** increase in the price of the underlying asset leads to a $0.50 increase in the option's price.
- Therefore, *the new price of the Call option* will be:

New Price = Old Price + (Old Δ × Change in underlying price) = $5 + (0,50 × $1) = $5,50

If the stock price rises to $101, the Call option with a Delta of 0.50 will increase by $0.50, bringing the option's price from $5 to $5.50. With the new Gamma of 0.10, the Call's Delta shifts from 0.50 to 0.60.

Gamma is significantly influenced by the time to expiration. As expiration approaches, Gamma tends to increase, making the option's Delta more sensitive to changes in the underlying asset's price.

For example, if we approach expiration and the Gamma of the Call option increases to 0.15, the Delta would change more rapidly. If the stock price rises by another $1, the new Delta of the Call option would become:

New Δ = 0,60 + 0,15 = 0,75

This implies a greater responsiveness of the option's price to movements in the underlying, increasing the risk and potential volatility of the option's price.

At-the-Money options have the highest Gamma, meaning their Delta is most sensitive to changes in the underlying asset's price. In contrast, In-the-Money and Out-of-the-Money options have lower Gamma values, suggesting that their Delta is less sensitive to price movements.

Gamma affects option prices in two significant ways:

1. It contributes to the overall risk associated with an options position. Higher Gamma values imply a greater potential for rapid changes in an option's Delta, leading to higher volatility and price risk.
2. Gamma influences the rate of options decay. As an option approaches expiration, Gamma tends to increase, causing faster changes in Delta. This means that the option's value can change more quickly as the underlying asset's price moves. Therefore, options with higher Gamma values are subject to greater time decay, particularly as they near expiration.

Traders anticipating significant price movements or an increase in underlying volatility might opt for long Gamma strategies. These strategies involve buying options with high Gamma values. If the anticipated price movement occurs, the rapid change in Delta can lead to substantial profits. However, it is crucial to manage risk carefully, as options with high Gamma values can also incur significant losses if the price movement does not materialise, making them unsuitable for inexperienced traders.

The relationship between Gamma and volatility is crucial. When volatility is low, the Gamma of At-the-Money options is high, while for In-the-Money and Out-of-the-Money options, it tends towards zero. With high volatility, Gamma tends to be more stable across all strike prices.

When implied volatility decreases, the Gamma of At-the-Money options increases. Conversely, when implied volatility increases, the Gamma of In-the-Money and Out-of-the-Money options decreases, as a greater possibility of further movements in the underlying asset is expected.

Gamma is a fundamental Greek that measures Delta's sensitivity to changes in the underlying asset's price. Understanding Gamma and its impact can help traders better manage risk and make more informed trading decisions.

Theta. Theta quantifies the rate at which an option's value decreases as time passes. It reflects the impact of time decay on an option's price. Theta can also be defined as the price surplus of an option relative to its intrinsic value, slowly affecting the value of the options. In practical terms, it indicates the gain (or loss) that occurs as time passes. Theta is represented by the Greek letter Θ and is typically expressed as a negative value.

Theta values are negative for both Call and Put options, indicating the gradual loss of extrinsic value over time. The magnitude of Theta depends on various factors, including time to expiration, volatility, and interest rates. It is important to note that the loss of an option's value is not a linear function, but follows a quadratic curve relative to time to expiration: it has a very modest trend in the period far from the expiration date, but increases as it approaches the option's expiry.

- **Call Options**: Theta represents the decrease in the option's value for each passing day. A Call option with a Theta of -0.05 implies that its value will decrease by $0.05 per day due to time decay. As the expiration date approaches, Theta tends to increase, indicating faster erosion of the option's value.
- **Put Options**: Similarly, for Put options, Theta measures the reduction in the option's value with the passage of time. A Put option with a Theta of -0.03 implies a daily decrease of $0.03 in its value due to time decay. As with Call options, Theta for Puts tends to increase as expiration nears.

Let me show you an example. Consider a Call option on a stock currently trading at $100, with a one-month expiry and a strike price of $100 (At-the-Money). Suppose the Call option is quoted at $5 and has a Theta of -0.05.

Imagine two days pass without any changes in the stock price. With this information, we can estimate the new value of the Call option.

1. Calculation of daily value loss:

- The Theta of the Call option is **-0.05**, indicating a daily loss of $0.05.
- After **2 days**, the total loss of value will be:

$$\text{Loss} = Θ \times \text{Number of days} = -0{,}05 \times 2 = -0{,}10$$

2. Estimate of the new option price:

- The initial price of the Call option is **$5**.
- After two days, the new price will be:

New price = Initial price + Loss = $5 + (-$0,10) = $4,90

Therefore, after two days, with no changes in the stock price, the price of the Call option decreases from $5 to $4.90, due to time decay represented by Theta.

The moneyness of an option, whether it is in-the-money, at-the-money, or out-of-the-money, influences Theta. At-the-money options generally have higher Theta values compared to in-the-money and out-of-the-money options. This is because at-the-money options have a significant time value component that is susceptible to time decay.

Theta is influenced by the level of market volatility. Higher levels of volatility tend to increase the extrinsic value of options, mitigating the impact of time decay. Conversely, lower levels of volatility can magnify the effects of time decay on option prices.

Theta may accelerate over weekends and holidays when markets are closed. This is because these periods represent additional time passing without the ability to trade the underlying asset. As a result, option prices can experience more significant time decay during these periods.

Options traders who understand and capitalise on Theta often adopt strategies that involve selling options, such as covered Calls or credit spreads. By selling options with significant time value remaining, traders can benefit from time decay as the options gradually lose value over time. This strategy can be profitable as long as the underlying asset's price remains relatively stable or moves in the desired direction.

Conversely, traders who anticipate significant price movements or changes in market conditions may opt to buy options with ample time to expiration. In this way, the impact of Theta can be minimised, allowing the trader to benefit from potential price changes without being heavily affected by time decay.

In conclusion, Theta is a fundamental Greek that measures the impact of time decay on option prices. Understanding Theta allows traders to gauge the rate at which options lose value over time, improving risk management and the formulation of more informed trading strategies.

Vega. Vega is an options Greek that measures the sensitivity of an option's price to changes in implied volatility. It indicates how much the value of an option is expected to change for each 1% change in implied volatility. Vega is represented by the Greek letter **v**.

Vega captures the influence of changes in implied volatility on option prices. Implied volatility reflects the market's expectation regarding the future volatility of the underlying asset's price. When implied volatility increases, option prices tend to rise, leading to higher Vega values. This is because higher implied volatility implies a greater likelihood of significant price swings in the underlying asset, which increases the potential value of the option. Conversely, when implied volatility decreases, option prices fall, resulting in lower Vega values.

Therefore, when you purchase options, the values of Vega are positive for both Calls and Puts. You will profit, regardless of the movement of the underlying asset, for each percentage point increase in implied volatility. Conversely, if you sell options, you are in a position of negative Vega and will profit for each percentage point decrease in implied volatility.

The moneyness of an option affects Vega. At-the-money options typically have the highest Vega values because they are the most sensitive to changes in implied volatility and tend to decrease as the strike price moves away from the current price. Additionally, Vega decreases over time.

Vega is generally higher for options with a longer time to expiration. This is because options with more time until expiration have greater exposure to potential changes in implied volatility. Consequently, options with longer expirations tend to have higher Vega values, indicating greater sensitivity to changes in volatility.

Here a practical example. Consider a Call option on a stock currently trading at $100, with three months to expiration and a strike price of $100 (at-the-money). Suppose the Call option is quoted at $5 and has a Vega of 0.20.

Imagine implied volatility increases from 20% to 23%. With this information, we can estimate the new value of the Call option.

1. Calculation of price change:

- The Vega of the Call option is **0.20**, indicating that for each 1% increase in implied volatility, the option's price will increase by $0.20.
- With a **3%** increase in implied volatility, the price change will be:

Price change = v (Vega) × Volatility Increase = 0,20 × 3 = 0,60

2. Estimation of the new option price:

- The initial price of the Call option is **$5**.
- After the 3% increase in implied volatility, the new price will be:

New price = Initial price + Price change = $5 + $0,60 = $5,60

Therefore, with a 3% increase in implied volatility, the price of the Call option increases from $5 to $5.60, due to the sensitivity to volatility represented by Vega.

Mathematically, Vega is defined as the derivative of the option premium with respect to volatility.

Vega is a fundamental Greek that measures the sensitivity of option prices to changes in implied volatility. Understanding Vega allows traders to better assess how changes in volatility can affect their positions, improving risk management and the formulation of more informed trading strategies.

Options traders who understand and exploit Vega often adopt strategies involving the buying or selling of options based on expectations of changes in implied volatility. For example, traders anticipating an increase in volatility may buy options to benefit from rising option prices. Conversely, traders expecting a decrease in volatility may sell options to benefit from falling option prices.

The Greeks I have examined in this appendix are the principal ones in the world of options. There are others that I have not mentioned since this is a guide for beginner traders and should provide a solid foundation upon which to build their future "profession" as options traders or, simply, to use options in various strategies in the markets they operate in and to diversify their portfolio.

WEB RESOURCES

APPENDIX B

Here are summarised important resources, some of which you have seen in this book, on options.

WEBSITE	LINK
Brokers	
Mexem	https://mexem.com/ – Offers a free trial for its brokerage services, providing access to advanced trading tools and low-cost trading options.
OptionsXpress	https://optionsxpress.com/ – Provides a virtual trading account allowing users to practice options trading without financial risk.
Websites	
OptionAlpha	https://optionalpha.com/ – Provides free tools such as a backtesting engine, trade optimizer, and strategy scanner specifically designed for options traders. They also offer real-time data and insights.
SeekingAlpha	https://seekingalpha.com/ – Offers free financial news and analysis, including insights into options trading strategies, market trends, and stock movements which are crucial for options traders.
Market Chameleon	https://marketchameleon.com/ – Offers free options trading tools, including screeners, profit calculators, and volatility data. They provide extensive data on options flow, unusual volume, and earnings analysis.
OptionsProfitCalculator	https://optionsprofitcalculator.com/ – This free tool allows traders to visualize the potential outcomes of their options trades. It offers a straightforward way to calculate profits and losses for various options strategies.
PowerOptions	https://poweropt.com/ – Provides tools for options screening, analysis, and portfolio management. It helps traders to find, compare, and manage the best trading strategies.

Optionetics	https://optionetics.com/ – Offers educational resources and tools for options traders, including strategy guides, market analysis, and trading tools to enhance trading performance.
Stocks Earning	https://stocksearning.com/ – Provides data and analysis on earnings reports, helping options traders to make informed decisions based on company performance.
CBOE	https://cboe.com/ – Offers a variety of free tools and resources for options traders, including quotes, option chains, calculators, and educational materials.
BarChart	https://www.barchart.com/options/ – Provides free options tools including screeners, volatility charts, and options chains. It also includes market data and analysis specific to options trading.
Finviz	https://finviz.com/ – While not exclusively for options, Finviz provides free tools such as stock screeners and heat maps that can be very useful for options traders looking for potential trades based on market movements.
Follow me	
Website	https://tradingwithdavid.com/
X	https://x.com/tradingwdavid/
Instagram	https://www.instagram.com/tradingwithdavidoriginal/
YouTube	https://www.youtube.com/@tradingwithdavid/videos/
TradingView	https://www.tradingview.com/u/TradingwDavid/

Table 1 – Web resources

Options Glossary

Appendix C

Adjustment: the process of buying or selling instruments to bring a position Delta back to zero and increase profits.

All Ordinaries Index: the major index of Australian stocks. This index represents 280 of the most active listed companies or the majority of the equity capitalization (excluding foreign companies) listed on the Australian Stock Exchange (ASX).

American Stock Exchange (AMEX): a private, not-for-profit corporation, located in New York City, that handles approximately one-fifth of all securities trades within the United States.

American-style option: an option contract that can be exercised at any time between the date of purchase and the expiration date. Most exchange-traded options are American-style.

Amortisation: the paying off of debt in regular instalments over a period of time.

Analyst: employee of a brokerage or fund management house who studies companies and makes buy and sell recommendations on their stocks. Most specialize in a specific industry.

Annual earnings change (percent): the historical earnings change between the most recently reported fiscal year earnings and the preceding year earnings.

Annual net profit margin (percent): the percentage that the company earned from gross sales for the most recently reported fiscal year.

Annual Percentage Rate (APR): the cost of credit that the consumer pays, expressed as a simple annual percentage.

Annual rate of return: the simple rate of return earned by an investor for each year.

Annual report: a report issued by a company to its shareholders at the end of the fiscal year, containing a description of the firm's operations and financial statements.

Annuity: a series of constant payments at uniform time intervals (for example, periodic interest payments on a bond).

Appreciation: the increase in value of an asset.

Arbitrage: the simultaneous purchase and sale of identical financial instruments or commodity futures in order to make a profit, where the selling price is higher than the buying price.

Arbitrageur: an individual or company who takes advantage of momentary disparities in prices between markets to lock in profits because the selling price is higher than the buying price.

Ascending triangle: a sideways price pattern with two converging trend lines; the top trend line is relatively flat (resistance), while the bottom trend line (support) is rising. This is generally considered a bullish formation, since most of the time it will break out to the upside.

Ask: the lowest price of a specific market that market makers, floor brokers, or specialists are willing to sell at.

Assignment: when the short option position is notified of the long position's intent to exercise. The long position exercises and the short position is assigned. The long position has the right to exercise; if the trader chooses to exercise, the short position must oblige.

At-the-money (ATM): when the strike price of an option is the same as the current price of the underlying instrument.

At-the-opening order: an order that specifies execution at the opening of the market or else it is cancelled.

Auction market: a market in which buyers enter competitive bids and sellers enter competitive offers simultaneously. Most stock and bond markets, including those on the NYSE, function this way.

Automatic exercise: the automatic exercise of an in-the-money option at expiration by the clearing firm.

Back months: the futures or options on futures months being traded that are furthest from expiration.

Back-spread: a spread in which more options are purchased than sold and where all options have the same underlying asset and expiration date. Back-spreads are usually Delta neutral.

Back-testing: the testing of a strategy based on historical data to see if the results are consistent.

Balance sheet: a financial statement providing an instant picture of a firm's or individual's financial position; lists assets, liabilities, and net worth.

Bar chart: a chart composed of a vertical bar in the centre that shows the price range for the period, as well as a horizontal hash mark that identifies the opening price. By reviewing the chart alone, a trader can determine the high and low trades for the time period designated on the chart.

Bear: an investor who believes that a security or the market is falling or is expected to fall.

Bear Call spread: a strategy in which a trader sells a lower strike Call and buys a higher strike Call to create a trade with limited profit and limited risk. A fall in the price of the underlying asset increases the value of the spread. Net credit transaction; maximum loss = difference between the strike prices less net credit; maximum gain = net credit.

Bear market: a declining stock market over a prolonged period of time, usually caused by a weak economy and subsequent decreased corporate profits.

Bear Put spread: a strategy in which a trader sells a lower strike Put and buys a higher strike Put to create a trade with limited profit and limited risk. A fall in the price of the underlying asset increases the value of the spread. Net debit transaction; maximum gain = difference between strike prices less the net debit; maximum loss = net debit.

Bid: the highest price at which a floor broker, trader, or dealer is willing to buy a security or commodity for a specified time.

Bid and ask: the bid (the highest price a buyer is prepared to pay for a trading asset) and the ask (the lowest price acceptable to a prospective seller of the same security) together comprise a quotation or quote.

Bid-ask spread: the difference between bid and ask prices.

Bid up: when demand for an asset drives up the price paid by buyers.

Block trade: a trade so large (for example, 5,000 shares of stock or $200,000 worth of bonds) that the normal auction market cannot absorb it in a reasonable time at a reasonable price.

Blow-off top: a steep and rapid increase in price followed by a steep and rapid drop in price. This indicator is often used in technical analysis.

Blue-chip stock: a stock with solid value, good security, and a record of dividend payments or other desirable investment characteristics with the best market capitalization in the marketplace. Many times, these stocks have a record of consistent dividend payments, receive extensive media coverage, and offer a host of other beneficial investment attributes. This term is derived from poker, where blue chips hold the most value. On the downside, blue-chip stocks tend to be quite expensive and often have little room for growth.

Board lot: the smallest quantity of shares traded on an exchange at standard commission rates.

Bollinger bands: specific types of envelopes that use expanding and contracting values employed as a lagging indicator. This is accomplished by setting the envelope lines above and below the moving average equal to a value that varies with price. Commonly used settings for Bollinger bands include the 20-period exponential moving average, plus or minus two standard deviations, to create the envelope channels.

Bond: financial instruments representing debt obligations issued by the government or corporations traded in the futures market. A bond promises to pay its holders periodic interest at a fixed rate (the coupon), and to repay the principal of the loan at maturity. Bonds are issued with a par or face value of $1,000 and are traded based on their interest rates—if the bond pays more interest than available elsewhere, it is worth increases.

Break-even: (1) the point at which gains equal losses; (2) the market price that a stock or futures contract must reach for an option to avoid loss if exercised; for a Call, the break-even equals the strike price plus the premium paid; for a Put, the break-even equals the strike price minus the premium paid.

Break-out: a rise in the price of an underlying instrument above its resistance level or a drop below the support level.

Broad-based index: an index designed to reflect the movement of the market as a whole (for example, the S&P 100, the S&P 500, and the Amex Major Market Index).

Broker: an individual or firm that charges a commission for executing buy and sell orders.

Bull: an investor who believes that a market is rising or is expected to rise.

Bull Call spread: a strategy in which a trader buys a lower strike Call and sells a higher strike Call to create a trade with limited profit and limited risk. A rise in the price of the underlying asset increases the value of the spread. Net debit transaction; maximum loss = net debit; maximum gain = difference between strike prices less the net debit.

Bull market: a rising stock market over a prolonged period of time, usually caused by a strong economy and subsequent increased corporate profits.

Bull Put spread: a strategy in which a trader sells a higher strike Put and buys a lower strike Put to create a trade with limited profit and limited risk. A rise in the price of the underlying asset increases the value of the spread. Net credit transaction; maximum loss = difference between strike prices less net credit; maximum gain = net credit.

Butterfly spread: the sale (or purchase) of two identical options, together with the purchase (or sale) of one option with an immediately higher strike, and one option with an immediately lower strike. All options must be the same type, have the same underlying asset, and have the same expiration date.

Buy on close: to buy at the end of a trading session at a price within the closing range.

Buy on opening: to buy at the beginning of a trading session at a price within the opening range.

Buy stop order: an order to purchase a security entered at a price above the current offering price, triggered when the market hits a specified price.

CAC 40 Index: a broad-based index of 40 common stocks on the Paris Bourse.

Calendar spread: a spread consisting of one long option with a far-off expiration month and one short option with 30 to 45 days until expiration. Both options must be the same type and have the same exercise price.

Call option: an option contract which gives the holder the right, but not the obligation, to buy a specified amount of an underlying security at a specified price within a specified time in exchange for paying a premium.

Call premium: the amount a Call option costs.

Candlestick chart: that includes the price range for the day, as well as the opening and closing price. A candlestick bar includes a "body" bounded by the open and close for the period and "shadows" which extend above and below the body to the high and low prices for the period. When the "body" of the candlestick is dark (or red in colour charts), the closing price was below the opening. When the body of the candlestick is white (or green in colour charts), the closing price was higher than the opening.

Cancel (CXL) order: an order is used to eliminate a prior order that has not yet been executed. A cancelled order must be communicated by a trader to the broker and such an order is not executed or confirmed until the floor broker reports back that the trader is out of the trade. Understand that once an order has been filled, it cannot be cancelled, so a CXL order is really only a *request* to cancel. Therefore, you should not assume an order has been cancelled just because you enter a request to do so—wait for the confirmation.

Capital: the amount of money an individual or business has available.

Capital gain: the profit realized when a capital asset is sold for a higher price than the purchase price.

Capitalisation: refers to the current value of a corporation's outstanding shares in dollars.

Capital loss: the loss incurred when a capital asset is sold for a lower price than the purchase price.

Cash account: an account in which the customer is required to pay in full for all purchased securities.

Cash dividend: a dividend paid in cash to a shareholder out of a corporation's profits.

Change: the difference between the current price of a security and the price of the previous day.

Chicago Board of Trade (CBOT): established in 1886, the CBOT is the oldest commodity exchange in the United States and primarily lists grains, Treasury bonds and notes, metals, and indexes.

Chicago Board Options Exchange (CBOE): the largest options exchange in the United States.

Churning: when a registered representative performs excessive trading in a customer's account to increase commissions. This is deemed illegal by the SEC and exchange rules, since the registered representative is not seeking improved returns and does not have the customer's interests in mind.

Class of options: option contracts of the same type (Call or Put), style, and underlying security.

Clearinghouse: an institution established separately from the exchanges to ensure timely payment and delivery of securities.

Close: the price of the last transaction for a particular security each day.

Closing purchase: a transaction to eliminate a short position.

Closing range: the high and low prices recorded during the period designated as the official close.

Closing sale: a transaction to eliminate a long position.

Commission: a service charge assessed by a broker and his/her investment company in return for arranging the purchase or sale of a security.

Commodity: any bulk good traded on an exchange (for example, metals, grains, and meats).

Commodity Futures Trading Commission (CFTC): a commission created by the Commodity Futures Trading Commission Act of 1974 to ensure the open and efficient operation of the futures markets.

Condor: the sale or purchase of two options with consecutive exercise prices, together with the sale or purchase of one option with an immediately lower exercise price and one option with an immediately higher exercise price.

Consolidation pattern: a resting period where the price action is in equilibrium. Typically, price action narrows and the volume drops off while investors and traders attempt to get a better sense of the next move, up or down. Visually, a consolidating market may resemble a triangle or a rectangle.

Consumer price index (CPI): a measure of price changes in consumer goods and services. This index is used to identify periods of economic inflation or deflation.

Contract: a unit of trading for a financial or commodity future, or option.

Contrarian approach: trading against the majority view of the marketplace.

Correction: a sudden decline in the price of a security or securities after a period of market strength.

Covered Call: a short Call option position against a long position in an underlying stock or future.

Covered Put: a short Put option position against a short position in an underlying stock or future.

Cover the short: to buy shares of stock to replenish those borrowed from your brokerage to place a short sale.

Credit spread: the difference in value between two options, where the value of the short position exceeds the value of the long position.

Cross rate: the current exchange rate between differing currencies.

Cycle: the tendency for price action to repeat uptrends and downtrends in a relatively predictable fashion over a prescribed period of time. Price cycles are measured low to low, high to high, or low to high. Various types of measurements are possible.

Daily range: the difference between the high and low price of a security in one trading day.

Day order: an order to buy or sell a security that expires if not filled by the end of the day.

Day trade: the purchase and sale of a position in the same day.

Day trading: an approach to trading in which the same position is entered and exited within one day.

Debit spread: the difference in value between two options, where the value of the long position exceeds the value of the short position.

Deep in-the-money: a deep in-the-money Call option has a strike price well below the current price of the underlying instrument. A deep in-the-money Put option has a strike price well above the current price of the underlying instrument. Both primarily consist of intrinsic value.

Delayed-time quotes: quotes from a data service provider that are delayed up to 20 minutes from real-time quotes.

Delta: the amount by which the price (premium) of an option change for every dollar move in the underlying instrument.

Delta-hedged: an options strategy protecting an option against price changes in the option's underlying instrument by balancing the overall position Delta to zero.

Delta neutral: a position arranged by selecting a calculated ratio of short and long positions that balance out to an overall position Delta of zero.

Delta position: a measure of option or underlying securities Delta.

Derivative: financial instruments based on the market value of an underlying asset.

Descending triangle: a sideways price pattern with two converging trend lines; the top trend line is declining (resistance), while the bottom trend line is relatively flat (support). This is generally considered a bearish formation, since most of the time it will break out to the downside.

Discount brokers: brokerage firms that offer lower commission rates than full-service brokers, but do not offer services such as advice, research, and portfolio planning.

Divergence: when two or more averages or indexes fail to show confirming trends.

Dividend: a sum of money paid out to a shareholder from the stock's profits.

Dow Jones Industrial Average (DJIA): used as an overall indicator of market performance, this average is composed of 30 blue-chip stocks that are traded daily on the New York Stock Exchange.

Downside: the potential for prices to decrease.

Downside break-even: the lower price at which a trade breaks even.

Downside risk: the potential risk one takes if prices decrease in directional trading.

Each way: the commission made by a broker for the purchase and sale sides of a trade.

Earnings: the net profit for a company after all expenses are deducted.

Earnings per share (EPS): the net profit for a company allocated on an individual share of stock basis.

Elliott wave theory: a technical tool based on R. N. Elliott's work in the 1930s. Elliott believed the charted price activity of a market is the graphical representation of mass psychology. In other words, the Elliott wave theory organizes the seemingly random flow of market price action into identifiable, predictable patterns based on the natural progression of crowd psychology. Elliott wave theory is based on the premise that markets will move in ratios and patterns that reflect human nature. The classic Elliott wave pattern consists of two different types of waves. The first consists of a five-wave sequence called an impulse wave and the second is a three-wave sequence called a corrective wave. Usually, but not always, the market will move in a corrective wave after a five-wave move in the other direction.

End of day: the close of the trading day when market prices settle.

EPS Rank: an *Investor's Business Daily* list of companies ranked from 0 to 100 by the strength of each company's earnings per share.

Equilibrium: a price level in a sideways market equidistant from the resistance and support levels.

Eurodollars: Dollars deposited in foreign banks, with the futures contract reflecting the rates offered between U.S. banks and foreign banks.

European-style option: an option contract that can be exercised only on the expiration date.

Exchange: the location where an asset, option, future, stock, or derivative is bought and sold.

Exchange rate: the price at which one country's currency can be converted into another country's currency.

Exercise: the process of implementing an option's right to buy or sell the underlying security.

Exercise price: a price at which the stock or commodity underlying a Call or Put option can be purchased (Call) or sold (Put) over the specified period (same as **strike price**).

Expiration: the date and time after which an option may no longer be exercised.

Expiration date: the last day on which an option may be exercised.

Explosive: refers to an opportunity that can yield large profits with usually a limited risk in a short amount of time.

Extrinsic value: the price of an option less its intrinsic value. An out-of-the money option's worth consists of nothing but extrinsic or time value (same as **time value**).

Fade: refers to selling a rising price or buying a falling price.

Failed rally: the inability of a market to sustain an upward move, often associated with a pattern that does not resolve itself in an expected upward direction. The most typical evidence of a failed rally is diminishing volume.

Fair market value: the value of an asset under normal conditions.

Fair value: the theoretical value of what an option should be worth, usually generated by an option pricing model such as the Black-Scholes.

Fast market: a stock with so much volume that the order entry systems have difficulty processing all of the orders.

Federal Reserve System: the independent central bank that influences the supply of money and credit in the United States through its control of bank reserves.

Fibonacci series: a mathematical series used in the markets that is produced by adding two sequential numbers to arrive at the next number in the series. Starting with 1, the series is: 1, 1, 2, 3, 5, 8, 13, 21, 34, 55, 89, 144, 233, . . . This series represents common naturally occurring phenomena such as the reproduction rate of a pair of rabbits and decay relationships, among others.

Fill: an executed order.

Fill order: an order that must be filled or cancelled immediately.

Fill or kill: an order to buy or sell an exact number of units or none at all.

Financial instruments: the term used for debt instruments.

Fixed Delta: a Delta figure that does not change with the change in the underlying asset. A futures contract has a fixed Delta of plus or minus 100.

Flags: relatively short-lived, sideways patterns that form after a sharp rise or decline in price. They represent a pause in the current move that occurs at the approximate midpoint. As a result, these formations have measuring implications. By definition, flags are continuation patterns. The flag resembles a rectangle that is slightly trending up or down (similar to a parallelogram). The slope's direction is often the opposite of the move prior to formation. These formations typically take one to three weeks to form, with volume diminishing into the pattern.

Float: the number of shares available for public trading in the markets.

Floor broker: an exchange member who is paid a fee for executing orders.

Floor ticket: a summary of the information on an order ticket.

Floor trader: an exchange member who executes orders from the floor of the exchange only for his or her own account.

Front month: the first expiration month in a series of months.

Fundamental analysis: an approach to trading research that aims to predict futures and stock price movements based on balance sheets, income statements, past records of earnings, sales, assets, management, products, and services.

Futures contract: agreement to buy or sell a set number of shares of a commodity or financial instruments in a designated future month at a price agreed on by the buyer and seller.

Gamma: the degree by which the Delta changes with respect to changes in the underlying instrument's price.

Gap: when the daily range is completely above or below the previous day's daily range.

Going ahead: unethical brokerage activity whereby the broker trades first for his or her own account before filling the customer's order(s).

Go long: to buy securities, options, or futures.

Good till cancelled order (GTC): an order to buy or sell stock that is good until the trader cancels it.

Go short: to sell securities, options, or futures.

Gross Domestic Product (GDP): the total value of goods and services produced in a country during one year. It includes consumption, government purchases, investments, and exports minus imports.

Guts: a strangle where the Call and the Put are in-the-money.

Hammering the market: the intense selling of stocks by speculators who think the market is about to drop because they believe prices are inflated.

Head and shoulders (H&S): the head and shoulders pattern is probably one of the best-known, most reliable patterns. The pattern resembles the silhouette of a head with shrugged shoulders. Each outside peak, or shoulder, is about the same height, with the middle peak, or head, higher than both shoulders. All three peaks use the same support line (the neckline) and a specific volume pattern is seen when this reversal is valid. The pattern is not complete until there is a close below the neckline accompanied by increased volume. These reversals occur at market tops and are bearish. Price projections are possible with valid H&S patterns.

Hedge: reducing the risk of loss on an outright directional move by taking a position through options or futures opposite to the current position held in the market.

High: the highest price that was paid for a stock during a certain period.

High and low: refers to the high and low transaction prices that occur each trading day.

Highflier: a speculative high-priced stock that moves up and down sharply over a short period of time.

High-tech stock: stock of companies involved in high-technology industries, such as computers, biotechnology, robotics, electronics, and semiconductors.

Historical volatility: a measurement of how much a contract's price has fluctuated over a period of time in the past; usually calculated by taking a standard deviation of price changes over a time period.

Holder: one who purchases an option.

HOLDRS: stands for Holding Company Depositary Receipts, which are exchange-traded funds that hold baskets of stocks from specific industry groups. HOLDRS trade on the American Stock Exchange and can be bought or sold in lots of 100 shares. For example, investors can buy or sell Biotechnology HOLDRS (BBH), Semiconductor HOLDRS (SMH), or Oil Service HOLDRS (OIH). In all, the American Stock Exchange offers trading in 17 different HOLDRS. Options are also available on these exchange-traded funds and can be used to profit from trends related to specific sectors or industry groups.

Illiquid market: a market that has no volume; slippage is subsequently created due to lack of trading volume.

Immediate/cancel order: an order that must be filled immediately or cancelled.

Income statement: a financial statement that shows a company's revenues and expenditures over a stated period (usually one quarter or year) resulting in either a profit or a loss.

Index: a group of stocks that can be traded as one portfolio, such as the S&P 500. Broad-based indexes cover a wide range of industries and companies, and narrow based indexes cover stocks in one industry or economic sector.

Index options: Call options and Put options on indexes of stocks are designed to reflect and fluctuate with market conditions. Index options allow investors to trade in a specific industry group or market without having to buy all the stocks individually.

Inflation: increases in the general price level of goods and services; it is commonly reported using the consumer price index as a measure. Inflation is one of the major risks to investors over the long term as savings may actually buy less in the future if they do not return an amount in excess of price increases.

Inside information: material information that has not been disseminated to, or is not readily available to, the general public.

Institutional investor: a person or organization that trades securities in large enough share quantities or dollar amounts that it qualifies for preferential treatment and lower commissions. These entities are assumed to be more knowledgeable investors who are better able to protect themselves from risk.

Interest rate: the charge for the privilege of borrowing money, usually expressed as an annual percentage rate.

Interest rate–driven: refers to a point in the business cycle when interest rates are declining and bond prices are rising.

Intermarket analysis: observing the price movement of one market for the purpose of evaluating a different market.

Intermarket spread: a spread consisting of opposing positions in instruments with two different markets.

In-the-money (ITM): when exercising an option would generate a profit at the time. A Call option is in-the-money if the strike price is less than the market price of the underlying security. A Put option is in-the-money if the strike price is greater than the market price of the underlying security.

Intrinsic value: the amount by which an option is in-the-money. Out-of-the money options have no intrinsic value. Calls = underlying asset less strike price. Puts = strike price less underlying asset.

Inverse relationship: two or more markets that act totally opposite to one another, producing negative correlations.

Investment: any purchase of an asset to increase future income.

Iron butterfly: the combination of a long (or short) straddle and a short (or long) strangle. All options must have the same underlying asset and the same expiration.

Lagging indicator: a technical indicator can lead or follow price action. A lagging indicator will move in a bullish or bearish direction after the same bullish or bearish price move. The extent to which an indicator lags is dependent upon the "speed" of the indicator. Lagging indicators include moving averages, envelopes, and channels. Many economic indicators are also considered lagging indicators that follow the overall pace of the economy.

Leading indicator: technical indicators can precede or lag price action. A leading indicator will move in a bullish or bearish direction prior to the same bullish or bearish price move. It is important to note that leading indicators can provide false signals; therefore, price confirmation is important. Leading indicators include volume and momentum, among other oscillators.

Leg: one side of a spread.

Level II quotes: one of three levels of the National Association of Securities Dealers Automated Quotations System (Nasdaq). Level I, quotes provide basic information such as the best bids and asks for Nasdaq-listed stocks. Level II, data provides investors with more detailed quotes and information. Level II users have access to current bids and offers for all market makers in a given Nasdaq-listed stock. Level III is the most advanced level and is used by market makers to enter their own quotes to the system.

Limit move: the maximum daily price limit for an exchange-traded contract.

Limit order: an order to buy a stock at or below a specified price or to sell a stock at or above a specified price.

Limit up, limit down: commodity exchange restrictions on the maximum upward or downward movements permitted in the price for a commodity during any trading session day.

Line chart: line charts "connect the dots" of the closing prices. They offer nothing as to the price action in any given time period, but are useful in looking at the overall price direction of a stock or index.

Liquidity: the ease with which an asset can be converted to cash in the marketplace. A large number of buyers and sellers and a high volume of trading activity provide high liquidity.

Locked market: a market where trading has been halted because prices have reached their daily trading limit.

Long: the term used to describe the buying of a security, contract, commodity, or option.

Long-term equity anticipation securities (LEAPS): long-term stock or index options that are available with expiration dates up to three years in the future.

Low: the lowest price paid for a stock during a certain period.

Low-risk investing: a trade that is hedged for purposes of limiting price loss, as opposed to a directional trade where loss is unlimited.

Make a market: a market maker stands ready to buy or sell a particular security for his or her own account to keep the market liquid.

Margin: a deposit contributed by a customer as a percentage of the current market value of the securities held in a margin account. This amount changes as the price of the investment changes.

Margin account: a customer account in which a brokerage firm lends the customer part of the purchase price of a trade.

Margin call: a call from a broker signalling the need for a trader to deposit additional money into a margin account to maintain a trade.

Margin requirements of options: the amount of cash the writer of an uncovered (naked) option is required to deposit and maintain to cover his or her daily position price changes.

Marked to market: at the end of each business day the open positions carried in an account held at a brokerage firm are credited or debited funds based on the settlement prices of the open positions that day.

Market: used to refer to the entire stock market, a specific sector, or a specific asset, security, or commodity that is traded at an exchange.

Market-if-touched (MIT) order: a price order that automatically becomes a market order if the price is reached.

Market maker: an independent trader or trading firm that is prepared to buy and sell shares or contracts in a designated market. Market makers must make a two-sided market (bid and ask) in order to facilitate trading.

Market on close: an order specification that requires the broker to get the best price available on the close of trading, usually during the last five minutes of trading.

Market on open: an order that must be executed during the opening of trading.

Market order: buying or selling securities at the price given at the time the order reaches the market. A market order is to be executed immediately at the best available price, and is the only order that guarantees execution.

Market price: the most recent price at which a security transaction has taken place.

Market value: the price at which investors buy or sell a share of common stock or a bond at a given time. Market value is determined by the interaction between buyers and sellers.

Mark to market: refers to the daily adjustment of margin accounts to reflect profits and losses. In this way, losses are never allowed to accumulate.

Mid-cap stocks: usually solidly established medium-growth firms with less than $100 billion in assets. They provide better growth potential than blue-chip stocks, but do not offer as wide a variety of investment attributes.

Momentum: a measure of the rate (velocity) at which a security is rising or falling. When a market continues in the same direction for a certain time frame, the market is said to have momentum.

Momentum indicator: a technical indicator utilizing price and volume statistics for predicting the strength or weakness of a current market.

Momentum trading: investing with (or against) the momentum of the market in hopes of profiting from it.

Moving average: probably the best known and most versatile technical indicator, this is a mathematical procedure in which the sum of a value plus a selected number of previous values is divided by the total number of values. Used to smooth or eliminate the fluctuations in data and to assist in determining when to buy and sell.

Moving average convergence/divergence (MACD): this popular lagging indicator, also known as the "Mack-D," represents the difference between two moving averages with differing time periods. One is shorter (commonly 12 days) while the other is longer (commonly 26 days). The shorter one is referred to as the fast line while the longer one is termed the slow line. When a stock is in an uptrend, the fast line will cross over the slow line. If a stock is trending down, the fast line will cross under the slow line.

Mutual fund: an open-end investment company that pools investors' money to invest in a variety of stocks, bonds, or other securities.

Naked option: an option written (sold) without an underlying hedge position.

Naked position: securities position not hedged from market risk.

Narrowing the spread: refers to lessening the gap between the bid and asked prices of a security as a result of bidding and offering.

Nasdaq: National Association of Securities Dealers Automated Quotations system is a computerized system that provides brokers and dealers with the ability to trade approximately 3,300 securities over-the-counter. On average, Nasdaq trades more shares than any other exchange.

Near-the-money: an option with a strike price close to the current price of the underlying tradable.

Net change: the daily change from time frame to time frame—for example, the change from the close of yesterday to the close of today.

Net profit: the overall profit of a trade.

New York Stock Exchange (NYSE): the trademarked name of the largest and oldest stock exchange in the United States. The NYSE operates as an auction market in which orders are brought to the trading floor for execution.

Note: a short-term debt security, usually maturing in five years or less.

OEX: this term, pronounced as three separate letters, is Wall Street shorthand for the Standard & Poor's 100 index.

Offer: the lowest price at which a person is willing to sell.

Offer down: the change of the offer of the market related to a downward price movement at that specific time.

Off-floor trader: a trader who does not trade on the actual floor of an organized futures or stock exchange.

Offset: to liquidate a futures position by entering an equivalent but opposite transaction. To offset a long position, a sale is made; to offset a short position, a purchase is made.

On-the-money: when the option in question is trading at its exercise price. (Same as **at-the-money**.)

Open interest: the number of total outstanding contracts for a specific option or futures contract.

Opening: the period at the beginning of the trading session at an exchange.

Opening call: a period at the opening of a futures market in which the price for each contract is established by outcry.

Opening range: the range of prices at which the first bids and offers are made or first transactions are completed.

Open order: an order to buy or sell a security at a specified price, valid until executed or cancelled.

Open outcry: a system of trading where an auction of verbal bids and offers is performed on the trading floor. This method is slowly disappearing as exchanges become automated.

Open trade: a current trade that is still held active in a customer's account.

Opportunity costs: the theoretical cost of using capital for one investment versus another.

Option: a security that represents the right, but not the obligation, to buy or sell a specified amount of an underlying security (stock, bond, futures contract, etc.) at a specified price within a specified time.

Option holder: the buyer of either a Call or a Put option.

Option premium: the price of an option.

Option writer: the seller of either a Call or a Put option.

Order: a ticket or voucher representing long or short securities or options.

Order flow: the volume of orders being bought or sold on the exchanges.

Oscillators: technical indicators that focus on a variety of chart data, including price and volume. Oscillators provide insight on trending markets and are most closely associated with determining overbought and oversold conditions. Upper and lower fixed bands are incorporated into an oscillator graph, and these bands warn of extreme market conditions. Oscillators are also useful in sideways trending markets since certain oscillators will lead the price action and provide clues about a potential move from the sideways pattern, as well as the direction of that move. Oscillator movement relative to a midpoint line can provide trading alerts and signals.

Out-of-the-money (OTM): when an options exercise price has no intrinsic value.

Out-of-the-money (OTM) option: a Call option is out-of-the-money if its exercise or strike price is above the current market price of the underlying security. A Put option is out-of-the-money if its exercise or strike price is below the current market price of the underlying security.

Overbought: a term used to describe a security or option in which more and stronger buying has occurred than the fundamentals justify.

Oversold: a technical term used to describe a market or security in which more and stronger selling has occurred than the fundamentals justify.

Paper trading: simulating a trade without actually putting up the money, for the purpose of gaining additional trading experience.

Par: the stated or nominal value of a bond (typically $1,000) that is paid to the bondholder at maturity.

Perceived risk: the theoretical risk of a trade in a specific time frame.

Performance-based: a system of compensation in which a broker receives fees based on performance in the marketplace.

Points: in the case of shares, one point indicates $1 per share. For bonds, one point means 1 percent of par value. Commodities differ from market to market.

Point spread: the price movement required for a security to go from one full point level to another (e.g., for a stock to go up or down $1).

Position: the total of a trader's open contracts.

Position Delta: the sum of all positive and negative Deltas in a hedged position.

Position limit: the maximum number of open contracts in a single underlying instrument.

Premium: the amount of cash that an option buyer pays to an option seller.

Price: price of a share of common stock on the date shown. Highs and lows are based on the highest and lowest intraday trading prices.

Price-earnings (P/E) ratio: a technical analysis tool for comparing the prices of different common stocks by assessing how much the market is willing to pay for a share of each corporation's earnings. P/E is calculated by dividing the current market price of a stock by the earnings per share.

Principal: the initial purchase price of a bond on which interest is earned.

Private company: a company that issues private stock and is not publicly traded.

Public company: a company that issues shares of stock to be traded on the public market.

Put option: an option contract giving the owner the right, but not the obligation, to sell a specified amount of an underlying security at a specified price within a specified time. The Put option buyer hopes the price of the shares will drop by a specific date, while the Put option seller (writer) hopes that by the specified date the price of the shares will rise, remain stable, or drop by an amount less than the seller's profit on the premium.

Quickie: an order that must be filled as soon as it reaches the trading floor at the price specified, or be cancelled immediately.

Quotation or quote: the price being offered or bid by a market maker or broker dealer for a particular security.

Quoted price: refers to the price at which the last sale and purchase of a particular security or commodity took place.

Rally: a brisk rise in the general price level of the market or an individual security.

Ratio back-spread: a Delta neutral spread where an uneven number of contracts are bought and sold with a ratio less than 2 to 3. Optimally, a back-spread is placed at even or for a net credit.

Ratio Call spread: a bearish or stable strategy in which a trader sells two higher strike Calls and buys one lower strike Call. This strategy offers unlimited risk and limited profit potential.

Ratio Put spread: a bullish or stable strategy in which a trader buys one higher strike Put and sells two lower-strike Puts. This strategy offers unlimited risk and limited profit potential.

Real-time quotes: data received from a quote service as the prices change.

Relative strength: a stock's price movement over the past year as compared to a market index.

Relative Strength Index (RSI): developed by Welles Wilder, this oscillator is used to measure the strength of a security's recent price relative to less recent price moves it has completed. It is often used to identify price tops and bottoms.

Resistance: a price level the market has a hard time breaking through to the upside.

Retracement: the amount in which a market move is corrected. A retracement is usually expressed in percentage terms, so if the original move was 60 points and a 30-point correction occurred, we would say there was a 50 percent retracement of the original move (30/60).

Return On Investment (ROI): the income profit made on an investment, calculated by dividing the net gain or loss by the total cost of the investment.

Reversal stop: a stop that, when hit, is a signal to reverse the current trading position (i.e., from long to short); also known as stop and reverse.

Rich: priced higher than expected.

Risk: the potential financial loss inherent in the investment.

Risk graph: a graphic representation of risk and reward on a given trade as prices change.

Risk manager: a person who manages risk of trades in a portfolio by hedging the trades.

Risk profile: a graphic determination of risk on a trade. This would include the profit and loss of a trade at any given point for any given time frame.

Risk-to-reward ratio: the mathematical relationship between the maximum potential risk and maximum potential reward of a trade.

Round turn: procedure by which a long or short position is offset by an opposite transaction.

Running stops: when quoted, floor traders use these to move the market. When stops are bunched together, traders may move the market in order to activate stop orders and propel the market further.

Seasonal market: a market with a consistent but short-lived rise or drop-in market activity due to predictable changes in climate or calendar.

Seat: the traditional term for membership in a stock or futures exchange.

Securities and Commodities Exchanges: organized exchanges where securities, options, and futures contracts are traded.

Securities and Exchange Commission (SEC): commission created by Congress to regulate the securities markets and protect investors.

Security: a trading instrument such as a stock, bond, and short-term investment.

Selling short: the practice of borrowing a stock, future, or option from a broker and selling it because the investor forecasts that the price of a stock is going down. Same as *short selling*.

Sentiment analysis: an attempt to gauge investor sentiment by analysing the subconscious of the marketplace through the use of specific psychological market criteria.

Shares: certificates representing ownership of stock in a corporation or company.

Short: the selling of a security, contract, commodity, or option not owned by the seller.

Short premium: expectation that a move of the underlying asset in either direction will result in a theoretical decrease of the value of an option.

Short selling: the sale of shares or futures that a seller does not currently own. The seller borrows them (usually from a broker) and sells them with the intent to replace what he or she has sold through later repurchase in the market at a lower price. Same as **selling short**.

Single-stock futures (SSF): an agreement between two parties that commits one party to buy a stock and one party to sell a stock at a given price and on a specified date. They are similar to existing futures contracts for gold, crude oil, bonds, and stock indexes. Unlike actual stock, there is no ownership or voting rights contained in an SSF.

Slippage: the cost of the trade that is lost due to commissions and because of the spread between the bid price and ask price. Traders try to keep slippage to a minimum, which can be done by using brokerage firms with low commissions and by sometimes placing orders between the bid and ask price.

Small-cap stocks: up-and-comer companies that offer big rewards and higher risks. They tend to cost less than mid-caps and have lower liquidity. However, small amounts of media coverage can prompt big gains.

Smoothing: in trading, a mathematical technique that removes excess data in order to maintain a correct evaluation of the underlying trend.

Specialist: a member of the securities exchange who is a market maker trader on the exchange floor assigned to fill bids/orders in a specific stock out of his or her own account.

Speculator: a trader who hopes to profit from a directional move in the underlying instrument. The speculator has no interest in making or taking delivery.

Spike: a sharp price rise in one or two days indicating the time for an immediate sale.

Spread: (1) the difference between the bid and the ask prices of a security. (2) A trading strategy in which a trader offsets the purchase of one trading unit against another.

Standard & Poor's Corporation (S&P): a company that rates stocks and corporate and municipal bonds according to risk profiles and that produces and tracks the S&P indexes.

Stochastic indicator: an indicator based on the observation that as prices increase, closing prices tend to accumulate ever closer to the highs for the period. Its goal is to identify where the price closes relative to the high and low for the day.

Stock: a share of a company's stock translates into ownership of part of the company.

Stock exchange or **stock market**: an organized marketplace where buyers and sellers are brought together to buy and sell stocks.

Stock split: an increase in the number of a stock's shares that results in decreasing the par value of each share.

Stops: buy stops are orders that are placed at a specified price over the current price of the market. Sell stops are orders that are placed with a specified price below the current price.

Straddle: a position consisting of a long (or short) ATM Call and a long (or short) ATM Put, where both options have the same strike price and expiration date.

Strangle: a position consisting of a long (or short) Call and a long (or short) Put where both options have the same underlying asset and the same expiration date, but different strike prices. Most strangles involve OTM options.

Strike price: a price at which the stock or commodity underlying a Call or Put option can be purchased (Call) or sold (Put) over the specified period (same as **exercise price**).

Support: a historical price level at which falling prices have stopped falling and either moved sideways or reversed direction.

Swings: the measurement of price movement between extreme highs and lows.

Synthetic long Call: a long Put and a long stock or future.

Synthetic long Put: a long Call and a short stock or future.

Synthetic long stock: a short Put and a long Call.

Synthetic short Call: a short Put and a short stock or future.

Synthetic short Put: a short Call and a long stock or future.

Synthetic short stock: a short Call and a long Put.

Synthetic straddle: futures and options combined to create a Delta neutral trade.

Synthetic underlying: a long (or short) Call together with a short (or long) Put.

Both options have the same underlying asset, the same strike price, and the same expiration date.

Technical analysis: a method of evaluating securities and commodities by analysing statistics generated by market activity, such as past prices, volume, momentum, and stochastic.

Theoretical value: an option value generated by a mathematical option pricing model to determine what an option is really worth.

Theta The Greek measurement of the time decay of an option.

Tick: a minimum upward or downward movement in the price of a security. For example, bond futures trade in 32nds, while most stocks trade in 8ths.

Time decay: the amount of time premium movement within a certain time frame on an option due to the passage of time in relation to the expiration of the option itself.

Time premium: the additional value of an option due to the volatility of the market and the time remaining until expiration.

Time value: the amount by which the current market price of a right, warrant, or option exceeds its intrinsic value. (Same as **extrinsic value**.)

Trader: a client who buys and sells frequently with the objective of short-term profit.

Trading account: an account opened with a brokerage firm from which to place trades.

Treasury bill (T-bill): a short-term U.S. government security with a maturity of no more than a year.

Treasury bond (T-bond): a fixed-interest U.S. government debt security with a maturity of 10 years or more.

Treasury note (T-note): a fixed-interest U.S. government debt security with a maturity of between 1 and 10 years.

Trend: the general direction of the market. Markets have three trends: up, down, and sideways. These trends can be major (primary) trends, corrective (secondary) trends, or minor trends. Primary trends typically extend for a year or longer; secondary trends extend for three weeks to six months; and minor trends extend for two to three days to two to three weeks. Typically, the closing price is used for the trend line.

Triangles: a sideways price pattern in which prices fluctuate within converging trend lines. When a stock enters one of these patterns it is likely to experience a decline in volume as the pattern progresses. As the price range gets tighter, the ensuing move is likely to be explosive. Common triangle patterns include symmetrical triangle, ascending and descending triangles, and pennants.

Triple Witching Day: the third Friday in March, June, September, and December when U.S. options, index options, and futures contracts all expire simultaneously, often resulting in massive trades.

Type: the classification of an option contract as either a Put or a Call.

Uncovered option: a short option position, also called a naked option, in which the writer does not own shares of the underlying stock. This is a much riskier strategy than a covered option.

Underlying asset: a trading instrument subject to purchase or sale upon exercise.

Undervalued: a security selling below the value the market value analysts believe it is worth.

Upside: the potential for prices to move up.

Upside break-even: the upper price at which a trade breaks even.

Value stocks: stocks that appear to be bargains because they are price lower than their calculated worth.

Variable Delta: a Delta that can change due to the change of an underlying asset or a change in time expiration of an option.

Vega: the amount by which the price of an option changes when the volatility changes. Also referred to as volatility.

VIX: the CBOE Volatility Index measures the implied volatility of S&P 500 Index options. When it rises, traders are becoming more bearish and are worried about future market volatility. For that reason, VIX is sometimes called the "fear gauge." Low VIX readings are a sign of bullishness or complacency among traders.

VXN: the ticker symbol for the Nasdaq 100 Volatility Index ($VXN). The index tracks the expected (or implied) volatility of options on the Nasdaq 100 Index ($NDX).

Volatility: a measure of the amount by which an underlying asset is expected to fluctuate in a given period of time. Volatility is a primary determinant in the valuation of option premiums and time value. There are two basic kinds of volatility—implied and historical (statistical). Implied volatility is calculated by using an option pricing model (Black-Scholes for stocks and indexes and Black for futures). Historical volatility is calculated by using the standard deviation of underlying asset price changes from close to close of trading going back

21 to 23 days.

Volatility skew: the theory that options that are deeply out-of-the-money tend to have higher implied volatility levels than at-the-money options. Volatility skew measures and accounts for the limitation found in most option pricing models and uses it to give the trader an edge in estimating an option's worth.

Volume: the number of shares bought and sold on a stock exchange. Volume should increase as a stock break through a support or resistance level.

Whipsaw: losing money on both sides of a price swing.

Wide opening: refers to an unusually large spread between the bid and asked prices.

Wilshire 5000 Equity Index: a market index of approximately 7,000 U.S.-based equities traded on the American Stock Exchange, the New York Stock Exchange, and the Nasdaq Stock Market.

Witching Day: a day on which two or more classes of options and futures expire.

Writer: an individual who sells an option.

Yellow Sheets: a daily publication of the National Quotation Bureau detailing bid and asked prices.

Yield: the rate of return on an investment.

Zeta: the percentage change in an option's price per 1 percent change in implied volatility.

Made in the USA
Las Vegas, NV
11 March 2025

19420595R00119